Rainbow
Liberated Energy

Ven. Ngakpa Chögyam, born in 1952, was raised in Farnham, Surrey, and trained as an illustrator at Bristol College of Art where he gained a first class honours degree. A student of Buddhism since his teens he travelled to the Himalayas in the early 1970s to gain first-hand experience of Tantric meditation. Since then he has studied and practised under the personal guidance of several Great Tibetan Tantric Masters and completed a number of long retreats. In 1983 he became an Initiated Ngakpa (Awareness-spell person) and returned to teach meditation and give courses on the Tibetan Mystic Path at Buddhist centres and other venues. Currently he lives with his wife in Cardiff carrying on the tradition of the White Lineage (Tantric, non-celibate Shamanic Lamas). An authority on Tibetan art he lectures widely at art colleges and teaches Thangka painting. He is a healer, a professional counsellor, and works increasingly with psychologists and those in the caring professions.

The Tibetan Mystic Path

The *Tibetan Mystic Path* series looks at our lives from the perspective of Tibetan Tantra in a down-to-earth humorous way. It is written to make available powerful teachings that have long been obscured by cultural and academic barriers. Ngakpa Chögyam's work is a bridge between the most magical tradition of Tibetan Buddhism and the everyday realities and pressures of city life. The series is based upon the numerous courses, seminars and talks given by Ngakpa Chögyam since 1983 and reflects his determined interest in enabling people to make real use of Tibetan teachings rather than being overwhelmed or confused by them. For this reason, these books have been written with the intention that no one having read them will be left saying: "So what do I do now?" This series covers subjects that have intrigued and baffled readers since books on Tibet first appeared, and presents them in a way that offers us the possibility of changing our lives.

Rainbow of
Liberated Energy

Working with Emotions through
the Colour and Element Symbolism of
Tibetan Tantra

Ngakpa Chögyam

Element Books

BY THE SAME AUTHOR
AND PUBLISHED BY ELEMENT BOOKS

Great Ocean
An Authorised Biography of the Dalai Lama
with Roger Hicks

© Ngakpa Chögyam 1986
First published in Great Britain 1986 by
Element Books Ltd
Longmead, Shaftesbury, Dorset

Second impression 1987

ISBN 0 906540 92 5

Printed by Billings, Hylton Road, Worcester

Art-photography of cover rainbow by 'Mujo'
Cover portrait of author by Flaming-Rainbow

Designed by Humphrey Stone

British Library Cataloguing in Publication Data
Chögyam, Ngakpa
Rainbow of liberated energy: working
with emotions through the colour and
element symbolism of Tibetan Tantra.
(The Tibetan mystic path series)
1. Tantric Buddhism
I. Title II. Series
294.3'925 BQ8915.4
ISBN 0-906540-92-5

This book is gratefully dedicated to:

HIS HOLINESS THE FOURTEENTH DALAI LAMA OF TIBET
MY ROOT TEACHERS, THE MIND, SPEECH AND BODY
INCARNATIONS OF PADMASAMBHAVA:
HIS HOLINESS DUDJOM RINPOCHE
KHORDONG TERCHEN TULKU CHHIMED RIGDZIN RINPOCHE
KHAMTRÜL NGAKCHANG YESHE DORJE RINPOCHE
AND TO THE GREAT MASTER OF DZOGCHEN:
LAMA NAMKHAI NORBU RINPOCHE.

May the White Lineage thrive for the sake of
everyone everywhere.

Contents

Acknowledgements

In some ways acknowledgements are autobiographical and could or should be longer than the book – preparing to write them I realise just how much I owe to others. So, I apologise to those I must omit through lack of room (whose absence is in no way a value judgement) because the selection is based on emotional closeness. I affectionately acknowledge:

My dear wife Fruitbat Cutmore-Smith whose wealth of experience as a Feminist Psychologist has been an invaluable source of guidance and inspiration. Having introduced me to the fields of Humanistic and Transpersonal Psychology I have become aware of a very valid and workable bridge between Tibetan Tantra and life in this country. Her constant support and lively encouragement were vital for the completion of the book, not to mention her tireless correction of my appalling spelling.

My dear friend Flaming-Rainbow, pupil of Hawk Little-John the Cherokee Medicine-man, for his humour, generosity, enthusiasm and insightful critical literary appraisal of the text throughout its various stages. The stages were many and varied ranging from the wilds of west Wales and the peace and homely comfort of the Lam-rim Centre in Raglan where I hold courses, to exhilarating gleeful and fearful escapades among the remote places of the Himalayas where his supplies of imodium and stemetil proved invaluable. Rainbow's home is always full of people who come to see him and leave feeling happier and enriched by his company. His experience as a Shaman and a Practitioner of Medicine has been a valuable resource along with his irrepressible wit and verve – I owe a great deal to the insights he has given me in the fields of medicine and psychiatry.

My brother/friend Graeham Smith and his wife Jill who take

me for skiing holidays at their expense and ask me questions about life that aren't easy to answer. Thanks especially to Graeham for taking me to the top of a 'red-run' in the middle of a rising Cairngorm blizzard the day after I'd learnt 'basic-swings' – a great teaching on the nature of fear.

My Good Mother who never talked about tolerance, kindness or compassion but whose actions over the years have spoken louder than words. They reverberate in my life today in the living knowledge that Kindness is the only 'relative morality' that can change our lives in this world.

My Vajra brothers Ven. Gelong Thubten Dadak, Ven. Arnham Lama and Ven. Tsering Lama whose kindness, vitality, openness and comradeliness gave me a great deal of strength at times when it was needed.

Ven. Geshe Damchö Yönten my respected friend who has gently pulled my leg for the last ten years. Having asked me to teach at his Centre I have got much more back than I have ever given.

The late great Ven. Ani Tsultrim Zangmo who died in 1984 and whose personality will be sadly missed. Tsultrim stood alone in my eyes as a western person who (having taken Tibetan Nun's Vows) actually *lived* the Path and integrated it with humour and ease in a western environment. Her integrity, pragmatism, cheerful Cockney chuckle and the mischievous twinkle in her eyes remain with me. When Geshe Damchö and I threw her ashes into the wind accompanied by mantras from the top of the Sugar Loaf Mountain we didn't say, 'Goodbye', but 'Come back soon!'

My pupils, especially Andy Hicks (Kunzang Dorje), Su Graves (Dawa Khandro), Brian O'Donovan (Nyima Dorje) and Caroline Tresise (Dechen Khandro). Their honest forthright real-life questions drew out much of the main body of material that makes up this book – without them the text would be a little dryer and duller. Their openness, sincerity and kindness shine out as a significant teaching for me.

My friend Sue Parkinson who listened to and was always so much part of the text. Sue always understood the difficult passages, but also understood why other people wouldn't which helped fulfil my aim of keeping the text readable and accessible.

My first teacher, Derek Crowe, who externally taught me Illustration for three years at Bristol Art College, but who internally set my feet on the road to Tibet. Derek's motto 'Infinite Flexibility' facilitated the personal growth of many students who passed through the Illustration Degree that he ran.

Jamyang Norbu, one time Tibetan hippy, now tweed-jacketed playwright and admirer of Orwell, Director of the Tibetan Institute of Performing Arts. Thank you Jamyang-la for your friendship, delightful company, fantastic stories, integrity, intelligence, humour and for the 'Old Monk' Indian rum.

My counselling clients who have gallantly taken up the personal challenge of working with their emotions and from whom I have gained much.

I would also like to thank: Dr David Fontana, Dr Steve Glascoe and Sue Relph, Dr Mo McManus, Dr Pema Dorjee and Yeshi Khadro, Dr John Crook, Prof. Jack and Barbara Parsons, Mike and Meg Smith in Montreal, Canada for cutting through timidity, 5 Cram for sounds, Steve Young for re-appearing, Ann Rimmer, Jay Jones and Chris Broadribb for Chi and Poetry, Pete Goodridge for the skylight and for being my Teacher on the nature of roofs, Pete Davis for making the environment of Sang-ngak-chö-dzong possible and bringing it to life with the everyday sparkle of his Practice, Lesley Christensen for the shawl, Jo and John Shane for being who they are, Harry the Monk of Tushita, the nicest Occidental I met in Asia, Seng-gye and Rose Tombs Curtis of 'Mujo' for the cover rainbow, Andy and Katie White for always being there, Lee Bray for living it with a grin, Mary Carter, Francis and Juliet Deas for the Nga-chen and Chod-nga, James Low for the crazy wit and encouragement, and all my Vajra Family of Lama Namkhai Norbu Rinpoche's Dzogchen Community.

NGAKPA CHÖGYAM
Mcleod Ganj and Roath, Cardiff, 1985

Khamtrül Yeshe Dorje

Foreword to the Tibetan Mystic Path Series

Translated by
VENERABLE GELONG THUBTEN DADAK

My heartfelt congratulations go to my faithful student Ngakpa Chögyam Ögyen Togden for writing these books which are the Wisdom-Dance of the five Khandros.

I have known Chögyam for many years and we are very close. Our harmonious relationship is like that of Milarepa and Rechungpa. Chögyam has studied and practised diligently in the Tantric tradition of the Nyingma Lineage for many years and is very kind-hearted and dauntless.

It is, therefore, my earnest wish that the clarity of these explanations will help people free themselves from their sufferings. These explanations will be of help to those with or without a knowledge of the Path who I wish may become free from delusion and attain peace and happiness. I hope also that these books will be a source of inspiration and courage to their readers, helping them to discover their beginningless enlightened nature.

THE SEVENTH KHAMTRÜL LAMA,
NGAKCHANG YESHE DORJE RINPOCHE
McLeod Ganj, 1983

Introduction

It gives me great joy to be asked to write an introduction to Chögyam's new book. He is an extraordinary man, not simply because of the path he has taken into Tibetan Tantra, but perhaps because he is one of the happiest and most positive people I have ever known. In this book he gives an outline of some of the ideas that have helped him achieve this fortunate position, but I do not want to steal his thunder already!

About seven years ago, I began to dabble in meditation. I read a little Zen and had a brief, and I must say, rather fruitless flirtation with 'TM'. Then one day a friend mentioned there was a man living locally who might be willing to offer information about Tibetan meditation: "He's a bit weird, but I think you might get on with him." So I went round to see him, not really knowing what to expect. I was greeted at the door by his wife who ushered me into his meditation room. Alone in the room for a few moments, I stared in awe at my surroundings. Here in this front room of a Victorian house in the centre of Cardiff was a little piece of authentic Tibet. Across the walls, painted with a draughtsman's skill, were broad stripes of colours which I later learned denoted the symbolic colours of the five elements of existence. Butter oil lamps glowed gently. My medical training enabled me to recognise one or two implements in the room, such as trumpets made from human thigh bones and bowls made from human skulls. I was later to learn that such implements help remind us of death, a vitally important thing for us to do in this strictly limited life of ours. In fact, the room was neatly crammed with mysterious objects and pictures. I can remember vividly my first impression: clearly, here was a man who took his discipline seriously; it was obvious that he had put an immense amount of work into this room.

When Chögyam entered the room dressed in his full Tibetan robes, I must admit that I was a little apprehensive that his teaching would be too sombre and pitched at too esoteric a level. But the warmth of his smile made me feel better immediately, and at once I was treated to the most concise, yet comprehensive description of how to approach the subject of meditation I have ever heard. His advice had a powerful effect on me. Technical advice was delivered almost with a chuckle, and always at a level I could appreciate ("Look, if you're feeling exhausted and strung out, don't try to meditate, watch television instead. Do you watch Dallas?").

We quickly became firm friends.

A couple of years later, I persuaded the local hospital neurology department to perform on Chögyam an EEG, or brain wave activity scan. This wasn't difficult: there were several people who were fascinated to see if ten years of committed mental training would have any noticeable effects on his EEG readout.

To explain briefly, there are two main kinds of brain wave activity: beta waves which have to do with conscious thought or concentration, and alpha waves which are associated with relaxed or calm states. Now it is known that a number of factors influence alpha wave activity. Meditative states certainly do so; some drugs, like alcohol and cannabis, do to a lesser extent; why, even a hot curry will show a small effect. So I certainly expected to see some changes from the normal in Chögyam's readout.

As they attached the electrodes to his scalp, we watched the pen trace out the patterns of his cerebral activity in response to various instructions ... "Just relax ... OK now we've got some mental arithmetic questions for you ..." Puzzlement turned to astonishment amongst the observers who turned excitedly to one another. What was happening? Was the thing connected up properly? The head of department, who had remained in the background until now, shot Chögyam a quick, quizzical glance and leant over the EEG machine. She went through the instructions again, expertly fiddling with the array of dials on the machine. Her frown deepened as the pen steadily recorded the slow, even picture of complete relaxation. "It just doesn't do that," she said. "Eyes closed ... now open!" This is normally guaranteed to demonstrate a flick from alpha to beta activity.

I tried to appear cool outwardly, but inside I was dumbfounded. At last, with half the neurology department clustered round the readout, he was asked to 'be angry'. I think this phased Chögyam for a moment. He certainly looked a little confused. Then I suggested he might try a Tantric visualisation of an 'angry manifestation' of one of the Tibetan Awareness-Beings. Suddenly the pen went berserk, skitting about all over the paper. There was a sort of breathless feeling in the room as the electrodes were finally removed from his scalp. Relaxing afterwards Chögyam himself was quite modest about the whole thing. "If they had wanted to," he said, "my Teachers could have got that pen to write their names in Tibetan script."

Hard work, then, seems to bring results although in Chögyam's case, as I've said, one doesn't need an EEG to prove that. Chögyam's subject is the art of life: how to live with grace and humour in this great antheap of western society.

The techniques he teaches are very subtle, but they are simple too. As I believe this book will demonstrate, the ideas are not high flown and esoteric, but astonishingly basic and direct. They address the issue of how best to deal with the nuts and bolts of our day to day lives. Now read on. Oh, and if I hadn't mentioned it before, thank you Chögyam!

STEPHEN GLASCOE, MB, CHB, MRCGP
Riverside Health Centre, Cardiff
April, 1985

Clarity – Sel (gSal)

Opening

Our Being is a brilliant pattern of energies: a spectrum of possibilities.

We have the capacity at every moment to experience the 'open dimension' of our Being, but somehow, the Awakened Mind appears rather remote from where we find ourselves; confused and bewildered by our emotions.

Some of us may have attempted to take ourselves in hand by instigating a tyranny of the will. We suppress our emotions because we find all that welter of emotional energy somewhat inconvenient. Opening ourselves to free-flowing emotions seems rather dangerous – anything could happen: we could put ourselves at risk in a way that might prove too painful, we could involve ourselves in areas of experience that we might find difficult to handle. It could all become a little bit terrible: we might have to sacrifice certain comforts and securities. Somehow we would seem to have got hold of the idea that in order for life to be as smooth and undisturbing as we would like it to be, we need to be 'sensible'. We would appear to have generated the conviction that freely expressed emotions are rather disagreeable. We need to play it cool; in fact, we play it so cool that we make our world a little colder and our relationship with our environment becomes a little stiff and frost-bitten.

Using the same kind of nervous logic we may have arrived at the view that we should rise above our emotions. We may well be working towards rejecting them in favour of some form of pseudo-spiritual emotional sterility and impotence. We may be attempting to become some kind of rarified etheric but slightly bloodless being. We are untouched by the dynamic earthiness of life and are oblivious to our loss, because after all, "Who needs emotional depth in the stratosphere?" We find our bodies an encumbrance, we would like to fly away to some other realm where beings are constantly smiling – but you touch no one and no one touches you.

The suppression of the emotions and the deification of the will can seem very upright and proper. We imagine that we can make up for any lack of 'zing' with our enhanced efficiency. But all we manage to acccomplish is to wrap life neatly in cling-film – we have undergone some sort of emotional lobotomy in which all we have gained is the dubious and vaguely arid comfort of "feeling in control of the situation". This is rather like saying, "I know that life is a bit limited now I've decided to put myself in this wheel-chair, but at least I'll never sprain my ankle again."

On the other hand, we could be conspicuously unattracted by the timidity and shallowness of this sort of control. We could feel that living by whim and wild impetuosity are "what life is really all about". So we abandon ourselves to our impulses.

Life then becomes a series of juxtaposed extremes: pain and pleasure, agony and ecstasy, tragedy and comedy, boredom and obsession. We could be said to be relating to life through inten-sity, as if intensity held some kind of meaning in itself. We could view the tangles of our emotions, the highs and lows, as "the rich tapestry of life". But this is an appallingly romanticised cliché – a way of looking back at our pain in order that it appears to have been to our advantage, but a piece of flaccid verbiage when we are caught up in our pain.

With abandonment to impulse in search of intensity, life becomes very earthy indeed. We tend to experience the earth by falling down onto it; at times it seems as if we meet the earth at terminal velocity. The nature of our contact becomes explosive – the repercussions throw us off balance and the ricochets whine alarmingly around our ears. Contacts become head-on collisions and we sustain repeated emotional injuries. We become brutalised by our contact with Earth, and our relationship with all the Elements becomes extreme. This is obviously quite some-thing, a truly rich assault on our sensory being. But we feed on

this bombardment: we experience Fire and Water in direct conflict, we get washed out, burnt out, blown out and spaced out.
Then we experience Earth again in terms of exhaustion and
incomprehension: sensory overload – complete wipe-out.

Either direction, control or abandonment, avoids direct and
naked confrontation with the real nature of our energies. We
never actually experience ourselves or our world, our Being or
our sphere of perception. It is important to experience our emotional energies simply and directly. Our emotions are a spectrum
of fluid and fluent energies and their exploration is the purpose of
this book.

We may feel that we don't have the right qualifications to travel
any sort of mystic path. We may feel that we aren't the right
people for this kind of enterprise. We could even imagine that
'spiritual people' are somehow intrinsically different, as if they
had specialised spiritual organs that we lack. There could well be
notions proliferating that practices for realisation are for
'advanced beings', or maybe that certain personality types are
drawn to this kind of activity. We, on the other hand, are either
more 'down-to-earth' or too pedestrian.

Ideas of this kind miss the point completely, failing to recognise the unique qualifications of all human beings. Maybe we
have never considered that our emotions are reflections of our
awakened potentialities: a rainbow of liberated energy.

PART ONE

Going round in circles – Khorwa ('Khor-ba)

1

Miasma of Constricted Energy

Every emotion is an open-ended opportunity.

Every emotion, feeling or sensation we experience is an expression of enlightenment – a manifestation of our spectrum of radiant energies. But almost always our emotions are distorted reflections of those energies and arise as a result of the way in which we constrict their natural display with compulsive intellectual contrivance. Whether we freeze our emotions out or drown in them, there is always a connection with our intrinsic yet unmanifested enlightenment. If we speak of our enlightenment in terms of being human, we could say that whether we are awake or asleep we are still human beings – and if we are asleep we can wake up. To wake up means to realise that our confused emotions were nightmares and that our dreams however pleasant are only dreams. But our dreams have a connection with waking life and the 'style' of our constricted energy is dynamically linked to the unrestricted display of our liberated energies. This is the most positive thing we could ever hear. This really is good news. Good and evil as totally separate fields of energy do not exist. This means that *every* state of mind is open to liberation – no one is too good or too bad. Every moment is a possibility, every negative state of mind has something of the quality of an aspect of our naturally liberated state. Every thought, every feeling, every sensation or action *is* enlightenment – but we do not realise it. When we drink a glass of wine, eat a piece of cheese, wash the dishes, cook food, make love, go shopping or hit our thumb with a hammer, enlightenment *is there* – we are never separated from it. There is no need at all to look for enlightenment in any other place than where we are. It is there unrecognised in the moment Now. There is clearly a quality of balance being sought when we suppress our emotions. There is clearly a quality of openness present when we risk abandonment to the heights and depths of our feelings.

So why do we constrict our energies? What prevents us from recognising our enlightenment if it is beginningless and ever-present? How do we come to discover the stillness of balance and the vibrant creativity of openness within the same experience? In order to find and understand the answers to these questions for ourselves we need to gain a deeper understanding of what we are and how we function. This is not a matter for intellectual specula-tion – thinking will not really help us. In order to understand what we are, to realise our unconditioned nature, we need to become simpler in our approach. We need to discover Space. We need to allow Space for our experience *to be precisely what it is*. This may seem to be a rather outrageous statement and certainly mystifying unless we take the time off to question the nature of our experiencing. What do we find when we examine our experience? Maybe this would be a good point to put the book down and give it a try.

Well, if we've tried to examine the nature of our experience we may well have discovered something quite peculiar: that it's impossible to examine the nature of our experience without the method of examination becoming part of the experience. In fact when we examine the nature of our experience in this way, the process of intellectual examination becomes our immediate experience. If we look for the nature of experience with our rational mind we can never find it – we can only ever dwell within the limitations of the rational mind. The living quality of experi-ence exists only in the present moment. As soon as we analyse it we become involved in some sort of historical research. We've crept off into a chilly archive to examine pictures of sunny days when outside there's a real sunny day to experience at first hand.

This is the foundation of duality. When we operate in this way we are artificially separating experience into two fields, like talk-ing about bread and baking as two separate phenomena which doesn't make a lot of sense. We are attempting to say that percep-tion and what we perceive are independent as if we could take the bake out of the bread or the bread out of the bake. With this divisive

logic we create a kind of analytical distance from direct experience. When we separate experience into two fields which actually
constitute experience by virtue of their inseparability, we lose our
'Knowing' and end up 'knowing about'. Ultimately there can be
no division between perception and the phenomena perceived.
Perception and field of perception are mutually self-creating –
Enlightened Mind is divisionless. Perception and field of perception are completely and utterly interdependent and their fundamental indivisibility *is* the Nature of Experience. So this is the
answer to our question: all we find when we attempt to examine
the nature of our experience is our commentary on it.

We all value the qualities of immediacy and spontaneity and
we can all remember moments of magic in our lives when our
consciousness was naturally expansive, when there was a certain
sense of spaciousness, when everything just happened with a
certain sense of ease and wonder. At these moments, for one
reason or another, we've forgotten to mix pre-structured concepts with what we perceive. The first throes of being in love can
have this kind of effect on us. Our enlightenment is ever-present
and sparkles through from time to time – not something that has
to be artificially constructed, it is there to be discovered.

Experience is Total. Experience is what it is – all-pervasive and
immediate. It is infinite in nature and cannot be added to or sub-
tracted from without straying into falsified or indirect experience.
As soon as we divide experience into perception and field of perception we separate ourselves from experience. This is what is
known as 'ego', the condition of duality which in future I'm going
to call *distracted-being*. The word 'ego' has developed too many
implications to be of any real use in my experience, so in future
we shall be using the terms *distracted-being* and *Liberated-Being* as
opposed to 'ego' and 'egolessness'. 'Distracted-being' carries the
idea that our enlightenment and our unenlightenment are not
separate from each other. We never have been separated from
our enlightenment but only seem to be so from the perspective of
our obsessive attempts to divide experience.

So, because it is not possible to divide experience in this way, we put ourselves in a highly improbable situation – that of imagining that this division is natural to our Being. This is what is known as illusion or *indirect experience,* living in a dream world loosely based on *direct experience.*

Immediacy of presence within experience is our natural condition – the rest is the strange, lurid or lyrical gossamer of our dreams. However, it is in this complex self-created mirage that we happen to find ourselves – running circles around ourselves with our thoughts. This is not to say that there is no place for our intellectual faculties – they are very valuable to us and can certainly function brilliantly in their own sphere. The problem with our intellect is that we are conditioned to using it to distract us from direct experience. We are always judging our perception as good, bad or indifferent and in this bizarre compulsive procedure all freshness is lost. We're living on week-old crusts and try as we may to enjoy them it never really comes off. We can splash them with water and toast them and maybe with enough jam or honey they'd pass for food. But we know that we'd have been better off making the effort to buy some good fresh bread and saving the stale remains for the ducks whose style of appreciation is different.

Because our perception is contrived and therefore indirect, we create our own version of the world with our stylised perception and respond to it as if it were real.

We are rather like young children playing with dolls – but dolls which we actually expect to grow up. Children I think at least have some awareness that they're playing a game. Because of this expectation, our reactions, interactions and relationships can be severely distorted and inappropriate – no real experience, no real perception, no real response and no real world.

In order to allow space for experience to be precisely what it is we need to take some kind of holiday from grabbing. We need to loosen our obsession with relating to the phenomena of our perception as reference points. We seem to have a maniac compulsion to understand everything we perceive in terms of our working body of knowledge. We relate everything in terms of categories – how one thing relates to another and can be fitted into our system. We come to understand the world in terms of previous experience where objects or events gain meaning when we group them along with other objects and events we fondly imagine we comprehend. We seem to need to be confident about the world in terms of the consistency of what we encounter in it. It's a sophisticated game resplendent with devices for ensuring our continued distraction. This process even includes the uncomfortable anarchy of 'the unknown' which we label as 'mystery'. Once something has been labelled a 'mystery' it can be safely held within the horizon of our conventional comprehension. We could well burst out laughing and the whole structure would collapse, but instead we reassure ourselves that this is a reasonable way to behave. After all we must make sense of our world mustn't we. Mustn't we? We could spend a lot of time trying to convince ourselves and probably often do, but our world has its own sense and there really is no need at all to impose an artificially constructed one upon it.

The kind of sense our world makes is immediate and spontaneously apparent. We can embrace it, we can be embraced by it, we can dance, but only if we let go of our obsessional pre-ordained system of understanding. Our world is not static. There are no rules that can always be applied – each situation is fresh and new. So why do we imagine that we can pigeon-hole our experiences? Why do we want to reconstitute life in our own terms? Are we really so convinced that for life to be comprehensible at any level we need to squeeze phenomena through a grid of our own devising? Our questions are starting to become quite interesting and we find that the more that we question the more we discover about the nature of 'distracted-being'. It is rather bizarre to be talking about discovering the nature of distracted-being. If we are talking about our obvious condition – the way we are – there should, you could say, be nothing to discover – it should all be obvious. But there are many things that we don't understand about ourselves. Take the way we walk for example. We could ask ourselves how we walk, and maybe we would answer that we just do it – we put one foot in front of another and it happens. We could say that we learned as children, when we were helped by our parents to experiment with balance, and now it comes naturally as do all our other skills such as swimming, cycling or skiing. But if we think about it a little we have a vast range of skills. We have the skill of enjoying certain tastes, of listening to music or looking at paintings or films. Maybe we have never considered these aptitudes to be skills that we have learned. Some people would disagree that we have learned the broad range of our sensory perceptions, but we only need to consider the range of foods and drinks that are described as being acquired tastes to realise that this holds true for those things at the very least. When we think about walking which seems so simple to us it would be interesting to look at the work that has been done in the field of robotics where the process of walking has been analysed and mapped by computer. With the resulting information, scientists have attempted to parody human walking. The engineering complexity of what we may feel should be fairly simple is in fact so difficult that it is beyond current technology. In terms of mapping the articulation of the hip joint we find, for example, that a point on the hip, when traced through the passage of a few steps, traces a distended coil. The joints move both vertically and laterally and the theoretical mechanical joints that would have to perform that function as smoothly as the human apparatus operates could easily be the work of decades. There are thousands of delicately balanced movements co-ordinated through muscles, tendons and ligaments and the attempts to reproduce these movements show us just how fantastically complex this business of walking actually is. We just do it. So, we've been discussing our physical skills and the skills of our sense perceptions.

But what about the world of ideas? What about the structure of thought and the convoluted geography of our personalities? The world of ideas is more complex and also more subtle. If we put ourselves in the position of thinking about the way we think we have a tricky little number on our hands. We are obviously limited by our style or manner of thinking. Something apart from thinking needs to look at thinking, and this 'something' is the 'open dimension' of our Being – the discovery of Space through the practice of meditation that we shall be looking at in the next chapter.

To return to our questions and our exploration of this familiar yet somehow unfamiliar landscape of distracted-being. In a relative sense our Being is distracted from be-ing and strays interminably in a miasma of cross-referencing fictions – the compartmentalising, labelling and judging departments of our conceptual bureaucracy. We seem to feel it imperative to seek assurances from our world that we really exist. We are somehow in doubt about our existence and it disturbs us constantly. A lot of people would say that they do not doubt their existence at all – they're as real as the next person, they know that they exist and what is more, they are probably annoyed and insulted by the question. But this is not completely honest. Have we really insulted their intelligence, or is this denial a fear response? Why, if we are so convinced of our existence, do we continually seek assurances and proofs of it? We may deny that we do this and this is not so surprising because we might not recognise our everyday activities described in that way.

It's not that easy to see the way we live our lives as a doubting process because we are so geared into the machinery of our distraction that we imagine our acts and motivations to be 'natural'. This doubt is rather chameleonic: it takes on the hue and tone of every aspect of our mutable emotional colouring. But where does this doubt come from? The doubt of our existence is both an aspect of our enlightenment and the echo of our fear of Space. We seek assurances from life that confirm the unconfirmable: that we are solid separate, permanent and continuous. But nothing at all, nothing whatsoever that comes into existence, has these qualities. Our existence doesn't conform to these criteria and so we cannot succeed if we try to establish our existence in this way.

Thus, we subvert the Brilliant Immediacy of our Experience with our endless attempts to establish reference points. This is our big problem; we are fighting a losing battle and nothing will serve us as a reliable reference point so we may as well jack it in as a bad job. Phenomena are not solid, permanent, separate and continuous, so they cannot possibly afford us proof that we are any different. Everything we encounter in our lives is impermanent by nature and will have only limited duration in the course of time. Even if we encounter phenomena that outlive us we lose them when we die, and at our death we in turn are lost to our friends and lovers. Impermanence is not only a quality of phenomena in terms of duration, there is also the question of ownership and proximity. Our prized possessions may have many more years in them but maybe not in our keeping. Whatever we have may be stolen or sold because of a sudden shortage of money. More subtly there is the extent of our own interest. Our prized possession may remain with us as long as we live but it may not always be prized so highly. Fashions come and go and jumble sales are full of the clothes that people once wore with delight, clothes that look fairly new. Fashion is a Great Teacher of impermanence. I remember when I was in my early adolescence badly wanting a ten-gear racing bike like everyone else. But when I finally got one no one was very impressed because not long after the first motorbike appeared on the scene and my peers were deriding me with the fact that I could have hung on to the money a bit longer and put it toward a motorbike. So an object that I felt proud of one day was just a push-bike the next . Making our-selves feel solid, separate, permanent and continuous by constantly scanning the phenomenal horizon for reference points is a tricky business. The phenomena of our perception will only serve us temporarily in this capacity, so if we want to carry on in this way we sentence ourselves to life imprisonment – the continuous activity of replacing reference points. Life becomes not only a prison, but a very subtle personal torture chamber: we need to be always on the look-out for new reference points, checking up on old reference points and generally being nervous and ill at ease about the whole process. It sounds pretty dire to me – a lot of unrelenting hard work in our own private forced labour camp. I don't think life needs to be that hard.

In our attempts to establish reference points we react to the phenomena of our perception in three ways: we are either attracted, averse or indifferent. If we encounter anything that seems to substantiate our fictions of solidity, separateness, permanence and continuity we are attracted. If we encounter anything that threatens these fictions we are averse. If we encounter anything that neither substantiates nor threatens these fictions we are indifferent – what we cannot manipulate we ignore.

So what is left when these three methods of relating to phenomena fall away? What would experience be like without attraction, aversion and indifference? The answer to our question is that fundamentally this is not any 'kind of experience', this is experience – *experience as such*. We are completely present, open and free in the experience of whatever arises as a perception. In this totally Spacious condition there is neither attachment, manipulation or insensitivity. We're talking about Straight Experience, not some fancy cocktail overloaded with tinned fruit with some chintzy paper parasol stuck in it. We want to concern ourselves with the Essence – the straight shot of undiluted experience.

We rarely have a straight experience because almost invariably we have a vested interest in establishing reference points. We are either nervous about the way that things are going, or we are throwing caution to the wind. Both are methods of attempting to manipulate the world referentially.

Caution is calculated manipulation. Throwing caution to the wind is desperate manipulation. It may seem difficult to envisage recklessness as a form of manipulation, but we are only ever reckless as a 'last ditch stand' method of securing reference points. We stipulate the exact ingredients of our joys and sorrows and react in accordance with how far circumstances meet our predetermined specifications.

I remember when I was quite young playing mime games. One game was to act out being trapped in a glass box or some kind of science-fiction force field. I would pretend to feel the walls, push against them and bounce back off them in my mock attempts to escape. Finally, I'd break through and get into some other game. Another game was to scale the garden as if it were a mountain. I'd have to find imaginary footholds and crevices for my hands. Sometimes I'd really have to stretch for a ledge that was almost beyond my grasp – it was difficult but I'd finally do it. It was a great game and it was one that I would always win. I suppose that games can be enjoyable if we know that we are actually playing them, but when we don't and suddenly it becomes real we have trouble on our hands and life starts to get very serious. The problem seems to be that we aren't enjoying our games. Our games aren't really working out well. People never seem to want to play with us without changing the rules to our disadvantage. We keep having to protest about it saying, "Hey! That's not fair. I thought we weren't allowed to do that!" And mostly because we've forgotten that we are playing a game the idea materialises that "this is the real thing". It would appear that we would much rather climb mountains than take a stroll in the garden. This is all rather tragic. We spend so much time setting up base camp among the runner beans that we never get round to picking them before they're too stringy to eat. We never get to eat an apple fresh from the tree because we are so worried about the approaching snowstorm. We never get to lie in the grass and gaze at the goldfish in the pond because we've got to reach the shelter of the west-facing ledge before nightfall. We are so preoccupied with making sure that our crampons are correctly adjusted that we never get round to taking off our shoes and socks and feeling the grass between our toes. How can we ever approach a mountain when we find our own garden such an ordeal?

We cling to our pain as desperately as we cling to our pleasure. We seek security in safety or in intensity. We turn our pain into a reference point and use it to prove that we exist. At least if we are in emotional pain it pin-points us as people who are in a state of trauma.

We tend our pain meticulously through the familiar process of thinking about it. The more we think around our emotional pain the more we cripple ourselves with the artificial intensity of it. We create a conceptual scaffolding that ensures that our pain will not collapse. We wish it to continue to serve as a reference point. We could allow our pain to dissolve into the skylike openness of direct experience; but somehow we feel more secure with our pain as a reference point. It seems to prove something about us and to make us feel solid. The nature of that pain appears to be very real and familiar, to be something that we really know about. We are more at home with our obscurity, our restrictions, our miasma of constricted energy.

Intrinsic Space – Long (kLong)

2

Discovering Space

In order to be real, in order to discover ourselves in *Actual Experience*, we need to encourage some practice of non-referentiality. In Tibetan this is called 'Shi-ne', which means 'remaining undisturbed'. With the practice of Shi-ne meditation; it's really not that important to sit in the 'lotus', 'half-lotus' or even the cross-legged position. The most significant aspect of posture is that our backs should be vertical and relaxed. Please notice well – I'm not saying that our backs should be 'straight', but rather that we should neither slump forward nor lean backward.

There's a natural, comfortable position where the spine will balance in perfect ease, so we need to find that position by experimenting. Sitting in a good, solid and fairly upright armchair is fine and probably best for a lot of people, especially if we're not so young any more or if we're not as supple as we might like to be. I've seen people treat the 'lotus' position as if it were some kind of mystic attainment in itself, but it's only a way of remaining physically still, alert, stable and undistracted. Tibetans were brought up to sit without chairs, so we should remember that we're not as culturally acclimatised as they are to sitting in such a fashion.

If you feel unavoidably compelled to sit cross-legged, get yourself a piece of dense industrial foam that raises your buttocks high enough off the ground for your knees to hang comfortably below the level of your hips. Sitting in this way will ensure two things: firstly that you don't get 'pins and needles', and secondly that your spine will settle in its natural position. If you try sitting on a cushion you may find that your knees are too high off the ground in which case your legs will 'go to sleep'. That happened to me once many years ago at 'Samŷe-ling' in Scotland not long after I'd begun to practise Shi-ne. I stood up when the 'singing-bowl' was sounded at the end of the morning hour of silent sitting and had lost all sensation in my legs. The outcome was most embarrassing because I fell backwards and pulled one of the rare old Tibetan Thangka paintings off the wall. Fortunately it was undamaged, but the incident has remained with me as a reminder that we need to respect the limitations of our bodies. Another problem with having your knees too high is that you'll be unstable and you'll either slouch forward or you'll attempt to keep your back straight and end up with the dreaded 'mid-back pain' which you can well do without. If you have to strain to keep your back vertical *you're in the wrong position!* The spine is not straight but vaguely 'S' shaped, so attempts to straighten the spine, whatever their purpose may be, are no part of the practice of Shi-ne. All straining and stiffness should be avoided, as forcing your posture only causes strain and discomfort that will quickly prove to be very distracting. The less we can be distracted by bodily aches and pains the better.

I've met numerous people who've given up the practice of meditation because they just couldn't get past the pain barrier of trying to sit in a 'spiritual position'. This is a great shame and rather ironic to say the least, because the 'lotus' position was originally formulated as an aid to meditation. The lotus position keeps the knees lower than the hips and allows the spine to sit easily, but if the pain of either staying in that position or trying to get into it outweighs its advantages it's best to forget about it. So sit any way that proves comfortable but make sure that you keep your spine vertical and that your general posture keeps you alert. This is one reason why it is difficult although not impossible to do this practice lying down.

When you've got yourself comfortable, allow yourself to breathe naturally and easily. There is no 'special' breathing technique, just let your breath flow as it will. You may like to start with a few good deep inhalations and exhalations to make yourself fresh and clear. At first you should simply *find* the Presence of your Awareness *in* the inward and outward movement of your breath. If thoughts arise don't block them, just let them be. If thoughts drift away don't detain them or grasp at them, just let them go. Rest your Attention in the movement of your breath and if thoughts come and go, allow them to lap like a tide, allow them to be a background 'coming and going'. If you get caught up in a 'thought-story' and lose the Presence of your Awareness in the movement of breath, just return to it as soon as you become aware of having drifted off. Don't be angry or irritated with yourself – these reactions are just opportunities to indulge in referentiality. Just maintain an open, humorous and relaxed attitude. Expect nothing, be attached to nothing and reject nothing – just Be, Here and Now. The practice of Shi-ne is one in which we make the commitment for set periods of time not to become involved with our thoughts. We do not examine the content of our thoughts, we just let them come and go without deliberately forcing them out or feeding them in such a way as to prolong them. We allow our thoughts to arise and dissolve without any intellectual intervention. We sit in a comfortable way keeping an alert posture letting go and letting be, and then we see what happens. After some hours, days or months of practice we may find that *nothing happens*, which is when the fun starts and we may well never look back.

This practice of stilling the neurotic thought processes introduces us to a new dimension of ourselves in which there is a sense of Spaciousness. We can learn through the practice of Shi-ne that when we relax and loosen up enough, we begin to discover Space. When we can allow our thoughts to arise and dissolve without commenting on them or becoming involved in them, we discover that there is Space between the thoughts.

This is not an empty space, not merely an absence of thought, but a vibrant emptiness. An emptiness which is in itself pure potentiality. We can discover that all thought and indeed all phenomena arise from and dissolve into emptiness.

In Tibetan this *emptiness* is called 'Tong-pa-nyi', and is recognised as the Source or Ground of Being. It is this recognition of Space within the practice of Shi-ne that enables us to appreciate the nature of Direct Experience. The artificial division between perception and field of perception evaporates into Space. Direct contact and immediacy characterise our Being because we no longer feel the need to evaluate our experience within the framework of referentiality. Our Awareness is Present and Flowing with whatever arises in the field of our perception. Phenomena and Awareness of phenonema are an instantaneous occurrence.

Awareness is the Uncontrived, Unattached Recognition of the experience of *movement* – the Movement of the arising and dissolution of thoughts in the continuum of Mind – the appearance and disappearance of phenomena in the vastness of Space.

There is only that sheer exquisiteness of this Movement.

This is where we actually are – it is infinitely and infinitessimally subtle. It is completely ordinary, humorous and somewhat magical.

In terms of working with the emotions, the practice of Shi-ne is absolutely necessary. In order to work with our emotions we need to have sufficient Clarity to see what is happening: we need to become *transparent* to ourselves. Becoming Transparent to ourselves means that we have developed sufficient recognition of Space to be able to observe ourselves in operation.

We are no longer a mystery to ourselves; perhaps we could say that we have simplified ourselves, we have simplified the way that we perceive and respond. We experience straight pleasure and straight pain. It's not a complex or elaborate affair: we don't embroider our sensations. We don't underpin our image of ourselves with justification. We are not compelled to rummage through the cumbersome baggage of past experience in every new situation. We are discovering spontaneity and are no longer menaced or lured by anticipation.

The main reason that we sometimes find our emotions so difficult to understand is that we are unable to see clearly what is happening to us, we are not *in* the process of ourselves. So it's all rather opaque – as if we were attempting to look through ground glass. This obscurity is caused by the *frosting* activity of thought to which we feel so attached. My Teacher once gave me a singularly amusing and earthy example of the process of thoughts chasing thoughts in circles: "You have a pile of shit outside your door that the dog has left. It has hardened in the sun. As long as it remains undisturbed it won't disturb you. As soon as you start stirring it round with a stick, the stench of it drifts into your room and makes you feel ill. So let your thoughts come to rest and they will not distract you from your Awareness."

We are unable to observe our energies directly because we haven't discovered Space as the core of our Being. We need room to get a look at what is going on, and the arising of a more Spacious way of Being enables our natural Clarity to operate more precisely. In everyday terms we stop talking ourselves into misappropriating our own resources. We stop selling ourselves down the river for a handful of plastic buttons and coloured glass. We learn to take a break from over-reacting, we cease to add to our problems.

There are, relatively speaking, two kinds of problem: the ones that arise out of the random functioning of the universe – the ones that life seems to hand out gratuitously – and the ones that we are responsible for ourselves. The problems for which we are obviously responsible are those that have arisen from our attempted manipulation of circumstances. The more actively we try to establish reference points the more problems we create. These self-created problems arise when we refuse to accept our world as it is. We respond to what is happening to us in too extreme a way. I think at this point it would be fair to point out that acceptance of what is happening does not constitute political impotence. This is a commonly held misinterpretation and one that it is important not to make. We are part of our world and cannot operate in isolation. We are responsible to each other and should discharge that commitment through taking an active part where necessary in shaping the future for the peace, joy and freedom of all. So seeking liberation is not some devious right-wing conspiracy designed to keep people quiet, it is about opening ourselves and losing our limitations. It is about taking action with awareness, with freedom and personal responsibility.

So we're not talking about accepting everything that happens to us along with every aspect of the world as it stands at present. We are not becoming part of the mechanism for maintaining the status quo. Part of this world that we have to accept is our own energy and its very specific qualities – we must not brutalise ourselves because it's supposed to be 'spiritual'. It is up to us to create as conducive circumstances as we are able without brutalising anybody else: we must find our place in the world. This means that we must be aware of ourselves and the nature of our energies, and how they are intimately interrelated with the energy of others. It is no favour to anyone to allow them to abuse us, neither should we stand back oblivious to the plight of those who share our planet. Creating conducive circumstances involves planning and making efforts which in many respects is a dangerous game as far as our equanimity is concerned. But life is dangerous, so unless we embrace the monastic life we have to work with the richness of life with all its complexity, colour, joy, sorrow, decisions, dilemmas, setbacks, misfortunes and rewards. It is a fantastically fertile field of learning but we have to find the Experiential Space in which we can pursue plans very *lightly* and with a sense of humour. So in terms of acceptance we need to accept the success or failure of whatever we do with a wry smile – we need to "treat the two imposters just the same". With the discovery of Experiential Space we can let go of the emotional investment we put into all our plans and efforts and things will become a lot easier. The *lightness* of this approach is a manifestation of our developing clarity.

With the development of Clarity which arises from the growing awareness of the natural Spaciousness of our Being, the life problems that occur cease to get out of hand and we no longer add to them. Ultimately our life is our responsibility. Our problems are for us to handle and work through, so it doesn't do us any good at all to blame the state of our life on anybody else. Taking responsibility for our lives is an attitude worth cultivating. Obviously there are many situations and predicaments in our lives that we could accurately describe as having an *external impetus*. That means that somebody or something has created or caused a sequence of events that has unfolded to our apparent detriment – someone has done it to us. The landlord or landlady is kicking us out and we can't find anywhere to live. The powers that be have cut our unemployment benefit for no apparent reason. A tree has crushed our car on a windy night and the insurance company are telling us they're very sorry but that they can't compensate us due to the fact that it was 'an act of God'. We may try to tell them that we don't believe in God, but they just smile apologetically and say that they believe in God as a matter of company policy and, what is more, that the Almighty obviously had it in for our vehicle. We can't take responsibility for the fact that we are being attacked by some unknown assailant intent on rape or robbery. We can't take responsibility for being made redundant as a result of government policy or being crippled by some drunken hit and run driver. We cannot take responsibility for the natural life-span of those around us, our friends, parents, lovers, relatives and children. We cannot be responsible for many things, but we are responsible for how we feel about the things that happen to us. To work with our emotions we must take responsibility for the style of our responses. If our lover walks out of the door to be with somebody new, we are responsible for how we feel about that. We can't say, "You have broken my heart! You are responsible for the misery that I am feeling." We are sad because we are sad. We are sad because we don't want our life to change. So if we get screwed up with the concept of our suffering being caused by somebody else we may well start stamping and shouting. We could get into some terrible tantrums and act in a way that makes our whole situation worse. Rejecting responsibility in this sort of situation spawns jealousy, bitterness, resentment, recrimination and vengefulness. Some people may say that we have every right to feel these twisted emotions but I doubt if anyone would actually argue that these emotions get us anywhere or that they help us to return to some kind of equilibrium. In this sort of situation it would be more helpful if we considered that no one has done anything to us – they have merely done what they wanted to do because they want to be happy. The fact that the thing that makes them happy makes us miserable is a theme that runs throughout our history as human beings on this planet.

Accepting sole ownership of our emotions can make an enormous difference to our lives – unless we can accept responsibility for whatever we feel we will not be able to work with our emotions.

As soon as we can accept that we cannot justify our feelings we will be able to approach our feelings openly. We will be able to experience our emotions as they are rather than as if we had rehearsed them. We can realise the possibility of our Natural Unconditioned Responses.

When we start to find some event in our lives painful or when maybe we have experienced quite a series of calamities we should try to avoid involvement in the 'unfairness game'. If we don't like what is happening to us we should attempt to side-step the confusion we usually cause ourselves by saying, "This is unfair! I don't deserve this!" We should merely say, "This is what is happening". There is no great consumer-protection society in the sky we can go to, no 'life-dissatisfaction appeals tribunal'. We can't say, "Life isn't what I expected, I want my money back". This is it. This is what we have got, right here and now.

If the car we are driving is breaking down and we're late for an important appointment, our reaction to that situation is completely our own responsibility. If we become angry because it seems unfair to us that this has happened today of all days then we have complicated and intensified our initial feelings. We could probably further inflame ourselves by shouting at our vehicle and maybe also at ourselves for having allowed it to get into such a lousy state of repair. We could get into a whole heap of ugly recriminations about how we knew we should have had it serviced.

Then we could scan the irregular index of our memory for suitable people to blame. We seem to be so highly skilled at making our situation worse. These contrived emotional additions to our situation are the computer soft-ware of distracted-being.

So what do we do? We sit in our wretched car in complete emotional ferment. Time goes by. We try to telephone for help but the phone is out of order. At this point we either throw another tantrum or we get ourselves more wound up and increase our blood pressure for good measure. Finally we get to a telephone that actually works. We get through to the car association who promise to come out as quickly as they can. We give them very exact details of how to find the car but we can't remember how to spell the name of the obscure little village we're passing through – it seems very much like the name of some other place that could either be quite near by or in the next county. The person on the other end finally seems to get the picture and we head back to the car. A few steps down the road we check our watch; an idea hits us and we run back to the box but a local, having appeared from nowhere, is in there rapping leisurely. We despondently notice the neat pile of coins they have set up to pump into the slot for more time. At last we get into the box to try to apologise that we are going to be late, but it's too late there's no answer. Our friends must have already left for the restaurant.

Panic sets in! We wind ourselves up a bit more. We try to phone the restaurant but the line is engaged. We try again and again but the line remains obdurately engaged. The telephone box is like an oven and we're sweating like crazy in there. So we try to wedge the door open with our foot to get some air but the traffic roaring past is appalling – every way we turn there seems to be some new and more devilish torment. We manage to get through to the operator to have the line checked and sure enough there's no fault on the line, the restaurant is actually engaged. We try again but just hear that irritating engaged tone – there's probably some imbecile talking to a friend about something completely trivial. We can't hang on any longer because the repair van could be arriving at any minute. We rush back to the car, but it is impossible to relax as we sit there; we are just too strung out even to read the book that was fascinating us only this morning. So we just sit there and drum our fingers on the dashboard brooding on the ruination of our evening. The van is a long time coming. We start to become more agitated. Should we go back to the telephone box and ring again? Maybe we could give the restaurant another try... We start to get out of the car but there is this awful feeling inhibiting us – if we run to the phone the van is bound to turn up as soon as we're out of sight. We realise after a while that we've smoked all our cigarettes and now we seem to want one quite desperately. Maybe we could just call a taxi and leave the car there ... we drum our fingers on the dashboard as idea after idea chase their tails through our tormented consciousness. Now we're really quite angry. We could have been back and forth to the telephone box several times by now. But at long last the van rolls up and the mechanic is very courteous and friendly, our car is put right in ten minutes and we're off again.

This story could just go on and on couldn't it? We could all add great long tracts of our own experience to the tale. Maybe we could run through our abortive attempts to impress our dinner guest or itemise the louse-ups of the failed seduction where we almost put our feet in it as many times as a centipede could have done. So, maybe we get to the restaurant in the end. Maybe we are able to wind down and have a delightful time or maybe we are just so overwrought that we blow the whole thing and go home with acute indigestion.

This story could be as long as anybody's life, a long tale of irritation, anxiety, frustration, nervousness, fear and anger.

We need to learn to relax with whatever is happening. We need to develop a sense of humour. Real humour only arises with the development of Space which enables us to recognise the ridiculousness of our problems. When the character of our experience becomes more Spacious we develop the ability to *see* our frantic attempts to manipulate the world to what we imagine would be our advantage. We start to *see* the pattern of these frantic manipulative strategies as something artificial – something that we have not deliberately constructed. *Seeing* the patterns of distracted-being, and recognising them as such, is the beginning of Clarity. And, as we discover some greater degree of Clarity we become increasingly transparent to ourselves and able to work directly with our emotions. We are discovering Space.

Meditation – Gom (sGom)

3
View, Meditation and Action

In order to realise ourselves as we actually are we need to gain some understanding of exactly how we have distanced ourselves from Being. We need to explore the geography of distracted-being, because every aspect of our distracted-being is dynamically linked to our intrinsic enlightenment – our Liberated-Being.

This exploration progresses on three fronts. In the Tibetan tradition these are known as 'Tawa' – view, 'Gompa' – meditation and 'Chodpa' – action. We can begin to work with these Now.

We can develop our *View*. *View* means the uncharacterised way in which we see ourselves and our world. *View* in this sense has nothing to do with philosophy. That is to say: it is not a constructed conceptualised way of seeing the world – it is *Seeing the world* and is intrinsically effortless and uncontrived. *View* is the recognition that relating to our world referentially is an artificiality. *View* involves our ceasing to employ preconceptions as elements of our logical investigations of our situation. *View* is the recognition that logical analysis is limited and that intellectual comprehension is no substitute for direct experience.

The development of *View* is encouraged by *Meditation*, which in this context is the practice of Shi-ne: the discovery of Space.

Ultimately Meditation is not a fabricated state that needs to be artificially maintained. It *is* our Natural state and as such only needs to be Discovered. This is really quite hilarious that the method of discovery *is* the discovery, and that hilarity in itself is only possible because of our innate realisation shining through. Real Meditation is sheer Effortlessness, and Shi-ne is a way of approaching this state. It is a way of encouraging ourselves to dispense with the illusion that we are unenlightened.

View encourages us to gain direct experience through *Meditation*, and *Meditation* gives us confidence of *View*. *View* and *Meditation* are the basis of *Action* which is the dynamic of our relationship with the world. That is to say: how we respond when *View* and *Meditation* are present in the moment Now. *Action* is the endless and spontaneous dance ignited by precise sensitivity to whatever happens. We flow harmoniously with *what is*, wherever we happen to find ourselves. *Action* is not therefore a way of acting or being in our world, it *is* Being; Unrestricted, Uncontrived, Unconditioned and Unlimited. In the Tibetan tradition, these three, *View, Meditation* and *Action*, are the principal aspects of the Mystic Path.

In this exploration of the emotions we are dealing largely with *View*. In this development of our *View* we shall come to recognise the different patterns that evolve from referentiality – the different styles of distraction available to us when we distance ourselves from experience and drift into distracted-being. These patterns are pale but relatively painful imitations of our liberated energies. The pain that we experience arises from our continual struggle to maintain our illusion of solidity, separateness, continuity and permanence.

Actually, our non-liberation or non-enlightenment is a bit of a joke. It's as real as our 'having a drink' when we're no longer having a drink. Where or what is our 'having a drink' when we're no longer engaged in that pursuit? We cannot find it except by having another drink. We cannot even compare the 'having a drink' that is happening Now, and the 'having a drink' that happened before. One is an experience and the other is a memory. As soon as we try to make any kind of comparison of present experience and past experience, present experience also becomes a memory because it is no longer our present experience. Our present experience becomes one of intellectual comparison. As soon as we attempt to locate or describe Being we distract ourselves from Being. Being is Being, rather than this kind of being or that kind of being – being this or being that.

Being is not attached to reference points and does not rely for its existence on any style of perceptual cross-referencing. Trying to pin-point Being is like attempting to suspend time and move-ment – it's not possible so we might as well just Be.

Ironically, in order just to Be we need to engage ourselves in some kind of discipline because from our bizarre standpoint we apparently don't know how to Be. We always have some crazy notion that there is a special method involved in Being. But Being is methodless – it is just that the limitations of our foggy faculties cannot encompass such an idea, in fact we cannot cope with it at all. So we need to *feel* our way with delicacy, daring and determi-nation. We have to get used to non-method. The effortless spon-taneity of Being is discovered through the practice of Shi-ne – our introduction to Space.

Attempting to live as though we were enlightened without the lived experience of Space doesn't actually work. Trying to be unrestricted, free and spontaneous whilst divorced from the experience of Space from which that condition naturally arises is doomed to failure. It's like trying to hang-glide with a feather duster.

We are attempting to *Be* Here and Now. This is something interesting and practical for everybody: *View, Meditation* and *Action*.

Five – Nga (lNga)

4
The Five-coloured Rainbow

The five coloured lights that illuminate our Being are the quintessence of our emotions. They are also the quintessence of the elements (Earth/Water/Fire/Air/Space) that comprise our materiality and the substance of our world. We are going to explore the qualities of the elements in order to arrive at some understanding of our individuality – the personal dynamic of our Being.

The psychology of the Tibetan Tantras describes our world and our Being as perceptible in three recognisable ways. We are going to get to know these as the 'Three Spheres of Being'. It is important to remember that although we are talking about a three-fold division of reality they are an indivisible occurrence and divided only for the purpose of analysis. This kind of analysis resonates with our perceptual orientation as human beings. This is a way of helping us to relate to how we are and how we function.

We could say that we are viewing the same reality through different lenses. We have our standard lens which gives us eyesight magnification: when we look through the view-finder of the camera we see things at their accustomed magnification. Then we have a wide angle lens which enables us to encompass much more than our eyes are able to see at any one time, but everything we do see is smaller. At the other end of the scale we can see what the world looks like through a telephoto lens. We find that we lose our panoramic vision of the world but now we can home in on things. We become aware of details. At either end of the scale we see both a lot more and a lot less – the reality is the same but our vision is different.

We can slow a film down or we can speed it up, to make another analogy. Were we to speed up the performance of a dance company we would notice aspects of pattern that are only apparent when the passage of time as we know it has been condensed. We would become aware of spatial interrelationships, the pattern would develop qualities of rhythm and we would have some sense of the entire company as a unitary organism. Were we to shoot the same action in slow motion, the patterns of movement even as observed in terms of conventional time would cease to be apparent. We would, however, start to become aware of the delicate subtleties involved in the individual articulation of limbs. We would observe the tensing and relaxation of muscles, the rotation and oscillation of hips and the gradual and delightful unfolding of movements.

To extend our analogy further: we could zoom in for close-ups with our slow motion sequences, and we could wind back into wide angle for the high speed footage. Our visions of reality would seem even less alike. But these are not separate realities: every view and way of understanding reality is simultaneously and spontaneously present. There is no point at all at which we can say, "This is the *actual* reality, the others are distortions." All we can say is that this is the human vision according to our individual perception. We can only say that this is human perception as modified by our culture, class, age and gender. There are, it would seem, as many different realities as there are perceivers of reality.

So when we examine these three Spheres of Being, we must start by taking a look at what is completely and utterly fundamental – we must recognise some Sphere or Space of origination. This Space of origination is the first of the three Spheres of Being: the *Sphere of Unconditioned Potentiality*. This is the primary Sphere, the Primordial Space which is empty, but from which all things – all appearances arise as the *play* of energy. It is this Space that is the *Heart Essence* of everything. It is Space that allows the phenomenal world to manifest as such. This emptiness is the most intrinsic quality of *what is*, it is the *ground of what is*, of *suchness, is-ness, thing-ness – Being*.

Nothingness as the direct and powerful source of endless manifestations is difficult to relate to as a lived experience outside the

Spaciousness discovered within the practice of Shi-ne. We need to realise Space experientially as the Ground of Being before we can relate directly to ideas such as this. Meditation then is a way of allowing ourselves the Space to experience and actually comprehend Space. There is something rather uncompromising about this.

The intellect is totally out of its depth at this point, and we are left either with the experience of Space or without it. There are no half measures – in order to comprehend this vastness we have to let go of our experiential agoraphobia. There's no dipping our toes in to see if the temperature is right, because from the point of view of distracted-being the temperature is never right. There's no shallow end to shilly-shally around in – this is an immediate total immersion job. This water is so startlingly brilliant, clear and sparkling that it demands our complete participation, our total commitment – there can be no wallflowers at this party. We're either in there with it or we're outside in the rain. We must reciprocate the innate dignity of this Great Ocean, we must experience it fully. If we relax and let go completely we find ourselves in the water having dived in effortlessly and with natural grace. We no longer seem to have dived from some terrible height. We realise that this is our natural condition – *this is what is.*

Because this Openness is our natural condition it constantly nudges us. If we meditate, if we practise this Shi-ne, we encourage this Openness. Shi-ne is the practice of getting used to Openness. Through it we discover that we cannot relate to this Openness through the process of distracted-being. If we don't let go of this process when we dive into the shining water of enlightenment, the instant re-wind cuts in and we find ourselves back on the edge with some vague memory of wetness. From the point of view of distracted-being Space evokes terror. From the View of Liberated-being, Space evokes delight.

The quality of emptiness is that it is the inexhaustible source of phenomena. This Space generates energy as its primary display, in the form of the five coloured lights. This display is the *Sphere of Intangible Appearance,* the Sphere of Energy, of Light and Sound. The Sphere of Energy is the bridge between the absolute and the relative, between emptiness and materiality. This is the Sphere of magic and creative imagination, the Tantric world, the non-ordinary reality of the shaman.

The Sphere of Intangible Appearance is where the Tibetan Tantric practitioner engages in the alchemy of transmuting distracted-being into Liberated-Being. The Sphere of Energy is the essence of our materiality and the substance of our world. The world that we know is the third Sphere. This world which we perceive through our sense faculties, including our faculty of intellect, is the Sphere of Relative Manifestation.

We have these three Spheres of Being. The first is the Sphere of Unconditioned Potentiality, which is emptiness or Creative Space. The second is the Sphere of Intangible Appearance, which is the primary display of energy appearing as sound and light. And the third is the Sphere of Relative Manifestation which is the aspect of reality available to our conventional sense faculties – the evident substance of our world.

Real symbolism is not arbitrary. We cannot just say, "This is a symbol for that". There must be a real connection. Symbols are a spontaneous manifestation of what they symbolise. The discovery of a symbol is concomitant with Direct Awareness of the 'whatever' that is symbolised – symbols arise from the symbolised. If we invent a symbol through the process of intellect it is not a real symbol – it would have to be called something else; perhaps a cipher or a logo. There is a fundamental difference here – the mystic works in one way and the graphic designer in another. The mystic discovers symbols and the designer invents them.

Symbols are *windows* through which we can *view* the Essential Nature of our Being.

The symbols we are about to explore are not exotic in any way – they are not alien to our experience. We aren't dealing with 'deep mysteries'; we're looking at ourselves and at our surroundings. These symbols are not fantastic or elaborate geometric patterns and this could come as a disappointment to some. I hope that what I have to discuss may actually prove to be more interesting and useful than an analysis of specific mandalas which would lead us into the complexity that often makes books such as this only readable by the specialist. These amazingly rich and incredibly detailed symbols exist in astonishing variety in the Tibetan Tantric systems, but their Essence is of the greatest simplicity. So, here we will be looking at the Essence and what emerges from it which could be of help to us in our everyday lives. It is important to realise that symbols do not limit *that which is symbolised*. It's vital that we are able to relate personally to the symbols we explore. As we become used to working in this way we find that the field of symbolism evolves in a style that is increasingly personal.

We are dealing with a fundamental and essential level of symbolism and we are involved at this stage with something we can relate to immediately as being integral to our experience. We are examining the Elements that constitute our physical being, and their Essence: the five-coloured rainbow.

Sign – Da (brda)

5
Reading the Field of Our Energies

The symbols that radiate as a communicative display from each ray of the five-coloured rainbow are the warp and weft of our lives.

We should not get the impression that these five expressions of our Being are 'eyelid movies' or that we have to drill some quaint little hole in our foreheads to enable our 'third eye' to function. Ideas of this sort have more to do with science fiction or mystical fiction than anything else. Our own eyes are all we need – they are the primary organs of our Clarity and need to be *Open* to *See* the world.

Most of us will have heard the word 'mandala' (the Tibetan for which is 'Kyil-khor') and may be familiar with what a mandala looks like. Everyone at least has some vague notion of concentric circles and squares. Some of us may have seen them in books of Tibetan art where they appear in their most complex forms. But here we are going to look at the most fundamental aspects of Kyil-khor. I think it is important at this point to underline the fact that complexity doesn't always represent profundity – the origin is always of greater profundity than the complexity of its display.

Kyil-khor can be translated as 'circle', and the Sanskrit word 'mandala' means 'grouping' or 'association' which carries the sense that everything gathers around a central point of some kind.

The central point of the Tibetan Mystic Path is Space. The central point of some of the other religions of the world is a God or Creator of some kind. The central point of a political party is its political philosophy embodied in the prime minister or president. Around her or him radiate the chief ministers, around them the junior ones and so on. There are different departments, factions and committees set up to make reports on various issues – they all comprise the energy field of the political party. Everything operates in the same way. When we are young, we have our parents and our sisters and brothers who radiate around us. Then we have the close friends of the family who are always dropping in, the aunts and uncles, grandmothers and grandfathers and so forth. Then we have our more distant relations, the ones we might get birthday or Christmas cards from, but whom we might not see very often. I guess this might not be such a good example these days for some people, because times are changing and have already changed a great deal since the turn of the century. This close system of relatives is known sociologically as the extended family and we are probably more used to the nuclear family or even single-parent family set-ups, but none the less there are people who radiate around us.

As we grow older our own friends become more important to us, and in some instances when we live far away from our parents and relatives, and maybe if we have fallen out with them, our friends become our family. At some stage we may connect with a partner, possibly having children of our own. We develop a small circle of good friends, a larger circle of friends whom we see more rarely and then there are the ones who move away whom we write to. We have acquaintances, colleagues, workmates, landladies, building society managers, bank managers, local shopkeepers and the many other people who cross our paths briefly at parties or under other circumstances. There are the people we never meet or speak to, who none the less play some part in our lives. There are others still with whom it might appear that there is no connection but who share the same town, village or city. Our activities radiate from our house, flat or bed-sit or our friends' places and other locations we visit for other purposes.

Wherever we are is an area of our Kyil-khor. Whatever we are doing is part of the energy of our Kyil-khor. We are simultaneously centre and periphery of Kyil-khor wherever we are. We are the centre of our own and in the periphery of the Kyil-khors of others – it is a totally interpenetrating energy.

Even if we were in solitary retreat somewhere, we could not isolate ourselves – there would always be people thinking about us, wondering how we were getting along, wondering if we were going to be different when we came out: linking us to their Kyil-khors. Even if we attempt to eradicate our personal history and become anonymous it is impossible to be free of our interconnections. Even when we die our friends and children remember us in their photograph albums as part of their Kyil-khors.

It's a wonderful dancing energy – it's not possible to exclude anyone from our Kyil-khor or be excluded from anyone else's. Even if someone didn't like us we would remain within their field of energy. Even if they loathed or hated us it would make no difference; in fact we would figure even more potently in their field of energy.

Ultimately every Being is part of our Kyil-khor, our Field of Energy, and we are part of theirs. It is vital, therefore, that we recognise this or be working toward this recognition. We cannot really ever love ourselves if we are attempting to be exclusive – it is not appropriate or accurate because we are trying to do something that is not possible. True love is centre-less recognition of Kyil-khor and the practice of Shi-ne is what gives us a feel for this View.

This five-fold symmetry of symbolism permeates our artificially structured perception of our world or universe, enabling us to view the entirety of perceptual experience as Kyil-khor. Kyil-khors are apparent in terms of *centres* of Unconditioned Potentiality which spontaneously manifest the luminous fringes of our perception. Kyil-khor then is our experience, sensation or consciousness of happening to find ourselves in our world. Of finding ourselves in relation to symmetrically radiating sets of conditions, locations, atmospheres, times and constituent elements.

Each of the five expressions of Being is associated with a colour, an element and a formalised symbol. They are connected with seasons, times of day and with the cardinal directions. They are also associated with any aspect of the phenomenal world, such as types of landscape, climate and weather.

No aspect of our world can be excluded, so we come to understand that this is not just some arbitrary set of metaphysical abstractions to which we are unable to relate. These five Fields of Energy *are* the conditions, circumstances, situations, personalities, predilections, and interacting forces that constitute our relationships with each other.

The five Energy Fields that relate to the Elements (Earth, Water, Fire, Air and Space) are known in symbolic Female form as the five Khandros or as the Wisdom Sisters. We will get to know them a little better in the next chapter, and more intimately as the book proceeds.

So this is the magical prism of endless interconnection – Kyil-khor. There is no more profound Kyil-khor than who or what we actually are in our world.

This is Kyil-khor, the Irridescent Matrix of Being.

The system of Colour and Element symbolism presented here is Intrinsic to the Vision of Tibetan Tantra. There are many systems of colour, element and direction correspondences in the world and although there are similarities between them they are mainly not externally aligned with each other. This, however, is no cause for conflict unless we make it so, because each system (if it is an Authentic system Realised through Direct Visionary Experience) functions perfectly within its own context.

Now some people will say, when they're shown apparently contradictory systems, "Which one is true?" But this question betrays an absence of understanding of the nature of symbolism.

A symbol is an *interface* between Ultimate and Relative – between the Experience of Spaciousness and the cultural/personal context of the perceiver.

Let's take an example. Say that someone eats a peach which they enjoy very much. Say then that someone asks the peach eater what it was like. The reply might be, "Mmm, edible ecstasy!" This reply is the symbol of the peach eater's experience, but there could be many symbols for that experience – some could even sound contradictory, but the experiences of peach eating wouldn't conflict with each other. (We're speaking, of course, about the experience of people who enjoy peaches!)

The Tibetan Tantricas say that White is the colour of Water and is associated with the East – with anger and Clarity. But among the Plains Indians of North America, White is associated with the North and with the Buffalo who symbolises Wisdom. Among the Plains Indians the East is associated with the colour Yellow and the Eagle who symbolises Illumination and far-sightedness. In this system the colour Blue plays no part, whereas Black which is not used in the Tibetan Colour/Element system represents the West and the Bear of Introspection. Green is found in the South with the Mouse of Trust and Innocence. This Amerindian Kyil-khor is known as the 'Medicine Wheel' but unlike the Tibetan Tantric symbol no Central Pervasive Quality of Origination is described in terms of colour.

Is it possible to learn anything from looking at the differences between these two systems? I'm afraid the answer is no – we can learn very little indeed, and nothing that will be of any value in our lives apart from the pleasure inherent in gaining information. These systems aren't mutually exclusive, but if we attempt to mix or synthesise them we merely distort them. They each work within the context of their own functioning. It's not even a matter of choosing one, we can work with both or yet others (if we are that Expansive), but not at the same time in some dreadful stew.

So, it's impossible to give an answer to the question, "Which system is the true system?" They're all true inasmuch as they all function to help people grow; but they're all equally untrue because they're not the Real Experience, they only represent it. Symbols are not Ultimate, they're tied to time and place and as such rely to a certain extent on shared cultural experience.

This may make some people feel that symbolism is a waste of time, but that would be wrong. Symbolism is valuable if it communicates something to us. The nature of our lives is in itself symbolic of our Enlightened Nature, so symbolism can have a powerful effect in prompting our ability to Comprehend ourselves. It's quite possible for us to relate to the symbolic systems of other cultures if we feel out of tune with the symbols of our native cultures, but the symbolism of different countries can't be compared and contrasted to any useful purpose. Each system is unique and valuable in its own right as is every human language – every language has its own peculiar strength and emphasis. The English language is amazingly flexible, German is very logical and Tibetan is rich in subtle vocabulary on the subject of Mind and Magic. No language is 'the best' language, but different languages suit peoples of varied climates, histories and geographies in their own special ways.

The Chinese and Tibetan acupuncture systems, as well as their calendars, use elemental systems that have Wood and Iron as elements and leave out the elements Air and Space, but no one finds a problem reconciling these systems in Tibet even when the same elements may have different meanings in the respective symbolic systems.

Tibetan Lamas often disconcert people by their enthusiasm for the scientific view of the cosmos, but they have three separate cosmologies anyway – the Ancient Indian Mt. Meru Cosmology, the Bonpo Cosmology and the Cosmology of the Kalachakra Tantra – so a fourth alternative poses no great threat. Viewed in this light Darwin and Genesis could co-exist quite comfortably as Alternative Realities rather than being ideas in opposition.

In Tibet in the nineteenth century the Ri-me movement flourished and was heralded as a renaissance of Mystic Endeavour. 'Ri-me' (pronounced 'ree-may') is often translated as 'eclectic', but the more literal translation is 'without bias'. The Rime movement consisted of a number of conspicuously great Lamas who mastered the other Tibetan Lineages and became Masters of all Schools and Traditions – without bias. The Great Jamyang Khyentse was one such Master and was famous throughout Tibet. When he gave Initiations he always gave them in the exact style of the School of their origin. If it was a Nyingma Initiation he would give it as a Nyingmapa, and if it was a Sakya Initiation he would give it as a Sakyapa. I tell this story because it's important to point out that the idea of the Ri-me movement was not to mix the Schools but to treat them individually. There was no synthesis but all traditions were taught by these Masters in their characteristic style, without bias.

There were some lesser known Buddhist Lamas who would work in the same way with the Bonpo (pre-Buddhist) system, and vice versa with Bonpo Lamas. Ven. Geshe Damchö Yönten, a Lama of the Gelug School, once told me that monks of every School would come to his monastery to learn debate because his monastery was famous for it, so much so that Bonpo monks would also come.

Tibet like most places where there are people, had its share of problems with sectarian dispute and even violence, but the spirit of harmony and respect was by far the most pervasive influence. Because both Buddhist and Bonpo systems had the Teaching of Dzogchen (Great Completion) as their pinnacle, some Lamas would describe themselves as neither one nor the other but as Practitioners of Dzogchen.

So, symbols can be as varied as people and their native habitat. Because symbolic systems contradict each other doesn't mean that there has to be a problem. There's only a problem for those who feel safer entrenched in dogma, or for those whose interest lies in the intellectual study of comparative religion. But for the Practitioner who sticks to one system there are no such problems, and for the Practitioner whose breadth of Vision can encompass it, many systems can be accommodated and utilised within the terms of their individuality as circumstances require.

Seng-ge dongma the Lion-faced Khandro

6
Dancing in the Sky

I would like to introduce you to the Khandros.

The word 'khandro' mean literally 'sky-going-lady' but 'sky-dancer' conveys a spectrum of meaning that comes closer to the Essence. Dancing in this sense is something that we do with someone – the idea is that we ourselves are dancers with the Khandros as our Dance-partners.

Sometimes the Dance is smooth and elegant, sometimes it's a wild and furious stomp, and sometimes we can't quite seem to keep up – but this in itself is still Dance. The Dance never stops, so we can never say, "Hey, I think I'll just sit this one out."

The Dance is always changing. It can be stiff and graceless when one person is always trying to lead, and when both partners try to lead it becomes a battle or a war dance. Whatever happens it always remains Dance, but in our perception it can become very confusing.

Dance becomes spontaneously Self-Realised when it becomes effortless – when we unify with our partner and our feet hardly touch the ground. Our movement is beyond us both and we discover that we are being Danced or maybe that the Dance and the Dancer are indivisible.

Space in the Tibetan Tantric systems is understood as being female and because of this female imagery it is important to its practitioners. Female symbolism arises from Space because of its womb-like qualities – Space is an emptiness which is Essentially Creative and continually gives rise to the phenomenal world. Space is often called the Great Mother – the Womb of Potentiality. Women are held in high regard in the field of Tibetan Tantra; the Tantric practitioner Views and Realises Woman-ness as the Source of Inspiration.

Sky-going carries the meaning of 'having room to move', having room to observe ourselves and our mechanistic mannerisms. We talk about 'taking a look at ourselves' or 'standing outside our situations for a moment'. In order to See Clearly we need room, we need Space for our Natural Clarity to manifest. Without the recognition of our Intrinsic Space we remain with our faces pressed hard up against our confusion.

The Khandros are our *moments of intuition*, our recognition of Space. As soon as we experience even the very faintest glimmering of Intrinsic Space a certain Clarity is present and our perception develops some translucence – we become *transparent* to ourselves, and in that Transparence we catch glimpses of the futility of our structured habit patterns. Being able to catch these glimpses develops with the experience of practice and becomes a great inspiration to follow the practice through. This is the Khandro, the inspirational intuition that enables us to untangle our emotional jungle.

The Tibetan Tantric system is rich with anthropomorphic symbols which constitute aspects or qualities of our enlightened consciousness. The Khandros are an important part of this system of symbols, and a forage into the mystic painting of Tibet – the 'awareness-imagery' of Tantra would introduce us to many different kinds of Khandros. Some are serene, displaying the Open quality of Transmuted indifference. Some are joyous, displaying the Open quality of Transmuted attraction. Some are furiously Wrathful, displaying the Open quality of Transmuted aversion. There is Seng-ge dong-ma, the Wrathful Blue Lion-headed Khandro whose terrifying roar shatters the illusion of unenlightenment, and whose secret spell turns back evil incantations. There is Trosma Nakmo the Wrathful Black Mother who cuts off the root of attachment with her Thunderbolt cleaver. The Khandros are unlimited in variety and function, pervading the fabric of the phenomenal universe. The dazzling active function of spaciousness.

All these many Khandros arise as emanations of the five primary Khandros who *are* the *Play of the Elements* – the Kyil-khor of phenomenal existence. This is why in the Tantric terminology our entire universe and everything that functions as part of it is called 'the Wisdom Dance of the five Khandros'.

This Dance is instructive to the practitioner who is Open to receiving its Inspiration.

This Dance is our constant field of opportunity. Practitioners see the circumstances on their Paths as Khandros and as such they are Viewed as their best friends. Every situation holds these inspirational qualities for accomplished practitioners because they are aware of the *Empty Nature*, or the *Spatial Condition*, of themselves and the world that they perceive.

Our emotions are the Dance of the Khandros – the Wisdom-Sisters. To know them is to Love them and to Love them is to discover our Beginningless Enlightened Nature in the Endless Empty Nature of their Dance.

PART TWO

Yellow – Ser (Ser)

7
The Energy Field
of the Yellow Sky Dancer

The colour Yellow is connected with the Element of Earth, with the distorted energy of arrogance and with the Liberated Energy of Quality and Balance.

Earth is massive by nature, existing in monumental forms that make us gasp at their magnitude. The Himalayas, the Alps, the Andes and the Rocky Mountains dominate the cultures of the peoples who live amongst them. The Earth can be overpowering in its grandeur and magnificence and we could easily feel dwarfed by it.

Earthquakes display something of the forceful arrogance of the distorted energy of the Earth element. It crumbles the labour of years in seconds leaving a trail of ruin in its wake – Earth can be a staggeringly fearful energy.

Earth can be built up into gigantic monuments to project our sense of self-importance. We can build huge mansions sprawling room after room where subordinates perform their various duties at our behest. The cellars are full of wine which our servants could never afford to drink, and our kitchens and larders are stocked with the very best of everything – we've probably got some 'endangered species pâté' in there somewhere.

Or maybe we could be a business tycoon in a tall angular labyrinth of offices made of concrete, steel and glass. We would occupy the penthouse suite which is lavish and overplayed beyond the point of ugliness. There are too many ornaments of untold value – wonderfully crafted furniture that we hardly notice. Ostentation has become the norm, and any kind of inconvenience has to be removed quickly – we will not tolerate any kind of discomfort in our environment. If creating comfort for ourselves causes problems and hardship for others we shrug it off blandly: "That's their lot in life, that's just the way it is." The misfortunes of others seem to be none of our concern because, "It's just that some of us have it and some of us don't." We'd say that what we've got we've worked for, or if we've not worked for it then it has been our birthright. We continually issue directives so that everybody remembers just how important we are. We continually engineer situations in order to convince ourselves that we have every right to act in this way. We want our world to be luxuriously padded, we want every sharp edge to be cushioned so that we can recline in our sumptuous velvet smoking-jacket and bloat ourselves further.

Earth signifies the material world and the ways in which we attempt to manipulate it to solidify ourselves. We'd like in some ways to be made out of marble because really we're making a naive bid for immortality and omnipotence. But ironically this drive is based on our deep-rooted sense of poverty. Our reaction to confrontation with Intrinsic Space has been one of destitution. So, in order to camouflage this feeling of worthlessness we have to try to own the phenomenal world. I think we've probably all heard songs about young men being rejected in love who go off and become big-shots just so that they can come back and say, "If you want me you'll have to beg..." There's some sort of tepid melodrama going on as well in which the young man imagines that his former object of adulation will end up living on the breadline in some seedy dump with damp and fungoid walls. She's supposed to see his name in lights and curse the day she so foolishly rejected him. At that point I think she's supposed to blow the rent money on making herself look splendid in order to go round and say, "But darling, it was a terrible mistake, you know I've always loved you." Our hero then sees himself being in a very powerful position because he has the option of accepting her or casting her out with some sneering remark about the poor quality of her apparel. He usually does the latter but is supposed to enjoy toying with the idea a bit first. I don't think this ever really happens in the actual world out there – it's largely a male

Earth-neurosis phantasy. If the young lady wasn't attracted to his energy in the first place, she's hardly going to find his energy attractive later unless of course she has considerable emotional problems herself.

The Earth Element's distorted energy – the energy of arrogance – has a lot to do with power, prestige and status: we want recognition and dominion. We want to establish our security beyond a doubt by accumulating and hoarding anything that is held to be of worth. Our relationship with the world is based on exploitation and on the expansion of our territory. But no matter how large our empire becomes, we can't quite get beyond our fear of poverty so we create our own conflicts by becoming despotic. Our despotism then creates certain reverberations and interactions that intensify our sense of poverty when people rebel or when sections of our empire collapse. There is always this niggling doubt, this fear of poverty that has as its origin the whisper of a suspicion at the back of our minds that we might not really exist at all.

This distorted energy of the Earth Element doesn't simply manifest in this far-flung extravagant style, it manifests throughout the social structure. The empire-building obsession can be seen in any aspect of life. The acquisition of personal contacts in the art world, spiritual circles and commerce – each of these fields is riddled with social climbing, manoeuvring, winning friends and influencing people. Whether we're after a second car or a fiftieth Rolls Royce to drive past our blissed-out admirers with, makes little difference; these drives are based on an inner feeling of poverty – our energy is bankrupt.

There are all kinds of materialism, some of which we have discussed which are quite blatant and some which are more covert. Our arrogance, for example, can be the silent smugness that refuses to Open itself to other people. In this frame of mind we cannot be seen to allow anyone their own field of experience – we have to relate on equal if not superior terms in whatever is being discussed. Sometimes people are taken in by us, sometimes they're bored and frustrated, and sometimes if they have a little

Openness it just makes them sorry that there can be no real communication. This inability to admit lack of knowledge and this inappropriate assumption of confidence is a great problem because it puts us in a position where we rarely learn anything. We increase our own poverty because we have cut ourselves off and cannot tap into the richness of the world. We can't share experience because we are using our pride to cover over our poverty.

I suppose some of us may have been in the sort of situation where we've been in the company of unfamiliar faces. There's been a very interesting conversation going on to which all but one person has been contributing. We've noticed them sitting there silently smiling and we may have wondered what they had up their sleeve. When the discussion reaches some interesting areas that are maybe a little abstruse our person with the fixed smile will say, "You've all been talking a bunch of crap." Sometimes it might be true of course – there's a lot of intellectual masturbation that is also part of the Earth neurosis. But whether the statement is true or false it is just someone speaking their poverty. They've made an unsolicited remark which is out of context with the Energy of the other people who have been putting their views and ideas on the line.

This kind of arrogance-based statement often carries weight if the audience is sensitive and self-questioning. It's part of 'Christmas-cracker wisdom' to think because Ultimate statements are simple that they can be as easily understood. Saying, "Natural is easy and easy is Natural," is all very well, but you might as well say, "It's all words, man."

This extends into the sphere of religion in the form of bigotry, self-righteousness and moral snobbery. I suppose we have all met people who seem as if they have some sort of franchise on the truth. There is a problem especially with Eastern religions where the need to know a foreign language enables those with a strong Earth-Element neurosis to reinforce their impoverishment by using their linguistic abilities to wield power over those who need them or who are impressed by that sort of thing. It's rather tragic to witness the credulity of those who mistake comprehension of a foreign language for Wisdom or Clarity. I've watched people riding the spiritual gravy train through linguistic ability and have noticed that what should be a wonderful opportunity to give generously of one's talent for the benefit of others, too often is just a miserly self-inflating sham.

Pride and self-satisfaction are based on very shaky ground and are usually short lived because pride is built on the concept of permanence.

Our Intrinsic Space is always Teaching us, sparkling through from time to time in unexpected ways dissolving the conceptual ground of our pride. These are golden opportunities, and if we use them to experience the nature of the Energy from which pride arises we can release ourselves from the illusion of poverty. Our pride is precarious because it rests on maintenance of the status quo – flying in the face of change. At the height of our brilliant athletic career we could be cut down by a debilitating illness for which there is no known cure. The wonderful house that we took so long to build could develop subsidence problems that we had not calculated on. The intimate dinner party we threw could leave quite a sour taste if our guests got food poisoning. The book we have written which we are so excited about could be ripped to shreds by the critics and our credibility could be in tatters. Life is not geared up to allowing us to maintain our pride – things just don't work in that way. In the world of mass-media popularity we are mainly forgiven for a certain amount of arrogance whilst we are on top. But once our popularity is spent, our arrogance is seen very differently – it seems hollow and pitiful and we become objects of derision, ridicule and censure.

There are a few medieval stories about rags to riches and back again, so people have obviously been aware of this pattern for quite some time. There's a German tale along these lines called 'The Adventurous Innocent' set during the Hundred Years War. It concerns a young boy brought up in a forest by an old hermit who took him in as an orphan and cared for him. When he gets to the sort of age where most young people want to set about discovering who they are and feeling as if they want to start taking their destiny into their own hands, he decides to quit the contemplative life. He decides that he cannot renounce a world of which he has no knowledge, so he sets out to meet the world face to face and gets into the whole schemozzel with gusto. He's a good-natured young man with a spirit of enthusiasm and everyone likes him. He gets on well in the world without treading on anyone and really seems to enjoy himself. But no sooner has he climbed the ladder than some awful mischance flings him back down again. This happens over and over again because of the extreme instability of the times, rather than through any significant fault on his part apart from his love of life and its enjoyments. Eventually, sick at heart and wearied by the ways of the world, he gives the whole thing up and goes back to find the old hermit. By this time the old man is dead, so he buries him in the forest, puts on the hermit's robes and lives out his life peacefully in the cave where he had spent his childhood. In Tibetan terms the young man chose the Way of Renunciation, but that is not the only method of working. It is also possible to chose the Path of Transmutation and work with the patterns of life without atttachment to failure or success – this is the Path of Tibetan Tantra which we are discussing.

Since nothing is permanent or secure, pride and arrogance are encumbrances we could well do without. The only stable ground we can find is by *establishing Insecurity as our Security*.

Although Earth seems so very solid and substantial we are aware that it can be eroded – but still we concentrate our efforts on attempting to maintain our cherished sense of solidity. We will not tolerate our dictates being ignored – our arrogance is outraged by any disagreement or criticism. We would have these people punished and publicly humiliated for their audacity.

But the Earth cannot permanently be moulded; it has a tendency to crumble, slip and level out, as well as to thrust itself up as the gigantic mountain ranges of the world. It's delightful to remember that Tibet which is now the highest plateau in the world and which is in fact still rising, was once the bed of an ocean. The fossilised conches used as horns in rites are a strong reminder that change affects everything. The props that we create from the Earth are transient – change and dissolution are always undercutting us whilst we cling to the distorted Earth Energy neurosis.

The Liberated field of Energy of the Earth Element displays the glorious warmth and wealth of Earth which is inexhaustible and free to whoever needs it. Wealth and generosity go hand in hand because even if we have very little we can be wealthy and attract wealth if we have the spirit of giving. This spirit always enables us to find something to give. Even if we have nothing to give away we can be generous with our Time and Space. I remember always the hospitality and generosity of poor Tibetan refugees who would invite you gladly to share what they had. A smile or a kind word could at the right moment be the most valuable treasure that anyone could offer. Noticing a lonely person in a group and engaging them in conversation rather than feeling that it would be more important to us to socialise with whoever the inset happen to be. Telling someone that we like them. Taking an interest in someone else's ideas and life-style. Being prepared to share an experience. All these things can be acts of generosity and we could all enrich our lives and the lives of others. By cultivating the recognition of Intrinsic Space we are enabled to flow in that way.

Miserliness on the other hand is the partner of poverty. Because we have constructed ourselves with the neurotic energy of miserliness we feel that we never have anything to give and so no matter how much we have we remain impoverished. The primacy of our need makes us hypersensitive to loss of any kind.

The colour Yellow is associated with the richness of gold, the warm glow of amber and the lush treacling sunlight that sparkles on the burnished wheat and barley. We can see it in the opulence of sweetcorn and the tousled ears of rye, the sweetness of honey, the sumptuousness of butter and the richness of bananas and sesame oil. Alternatively yellow as a distorted field of energy can manifest as decay and death, putrescence, the colour of old paper and ageing skin – the colour of disease.

The formalised Tibetan symbol of this Energy-field is Rinchen, the wish-fulfilling gem – the exuberant magnanimous source of all wealth and sustenance. Rinchen is the source of all requirements and spontaneously supplies every need. Rinchen the multi-faceted jewel reflects light in all directions equally, showering the universe in a warm radiant glow.

The cardinal direction associated with the Yellow Sky Dancer is the South which is always warm and hospitable. Even the seemingly wealthiest of us appear to be able to draw sustenance from the Earth in very simple terms when we are on holiday – we just lie on the sand and soak up the sun. The sun tans us all equally and apart from the cost of getting to where it is actually shining, it is entirely free.

The Yellow Sky Dancer performs for us in Autumn in the time of the harvest when the trees are heavy with fruit and the bushes are bulging with all kinds of berries. Crops are being gathered in and grain is ground and milled into flour. Outrageous orange pumpkins are hung from the ceiling in nets for storage, later to make soups and pies. Preserves are bottled, jams made and wine ferments in kitchens in demi-johns and carboys bubbling merrily. There's an abundance of delightful food and a sense of nourishment and fulfilment pervades the air. Even if the fruits and vegetables are not picked their wholesomeness enriches the Earth through the process of rotting. Everything returns to the Earth as part of the cycle of enrichment and fertility. The Earth is a precious treasure-house and as such supplies all our physical needs.

This field of Energy is associated with mid morning when the day is full of promise – pregnant with possibilities. The grass is soft and springy under our feet being still slightly moist. The sun is climbing in the sky and the woods are full of tasty surprises – hazel-nuts, chestnuts and mushrooms that spring up magically from nowhere.

The kind of wealth we are discussing is reflected by our environment but is *Central to our Being*. We really do have all that we need in the discovery of Intrinsic Space. With this recognition we could realise that we are already totally secure in the Primordial Nature of our Being – we have within us the Wisdom of Equanimity and are free of attachment.

Mind is sufficient to itself and so is our world. Mind requires nothing but is the Ground of Everything – the Unemptiable Source of phenomena.

White – Kar (dKar)

8
The Energy Field
of the White Sky Dancer

The colour White is connected to the Element of Water; to the distorted energy of anger and the Liberated Energy of Clarity.

Water can be opaque, surging with numberless bubbles as it thrashes against projecting rocks or as it rolls and tumbles at the feet of cliffs. The tremendous power of 'white-water' has to be treated with considerable caution – its current of aggression is lethal. The river Be-as in Manali in the Himalayas is the most dramatic example I have ever encountered. I remember when I was staying there near the Gompa (meditation-place) of Apo Rinpoche, that there was always the temptation to venture into it for a swim. But I knew that I'd be crushed to death long before I had time to drown. There were some side pools protected by huge boulders from the main current that I used to sit on in order to feel the coolness of the vaporised spray as I tried to allow my awareness to blend with the roaring waters. The spray from the rocks, the glacial boulders that lay in the main current of the Be-as, was so violent that even a shutter speed setting of a two-thousandth of a second was not quick enough to freeze the froth. But in its rampant ferocity there was a clear, crisp and immaculate beauty that seemed completely pure – utterly unadulterated.

Water can also boil and spit with fury in a cauldron or in a geothermal spring. It can froth and spray with the vitriolic disregard of rage with no sense of self-control. Water displays the qualities of anger in a whole variety of ways – we need only walk along the seashore to observe fragments of wreckage; the battered remains; the flotsam and jetsam of who-knows-what. But anger is not always so uninhibited, sometimes it can be icy, the cold bitter anger of calculating destructiveness. We may seem to be outwardly controlled, but internally atomic war is in progress. Our every action is accurately and finely determined to have some very specific hurtful effect. Our motives have the sharpness and lacerating precision of broken glass or fragmented ice. When water freezes it can be the instrument of severe surgical mutilation.

However anger manifests, it has the quality of sharpening our presence – we become almost one-pointed. When we get angry about something in particular, all those aspects of life that we usually find irritating, awkward or embarrassing melt away into some kind of blur in the outer margins of our immediate emotional memory. Our usual worries and anxieties no longer seem to provide us with such a distracting influence. The unpaid milk bill, the broken cistern in the loo, the fellow next door who plays his saxophones at all hours of the day and night (why does he always have to play 'When the Saints Go Marching in'?), the disorganised couple on the other side who leave mounds of festering rubbish outside their back door because they never seem to get it past the back gate for the dustbin men to collect. Somehow these things don't seem quite so horribly irritating any more if we are venting our spleen about something else.

Anger is a direct communication, an intellectual energy which is only concerned with its relationship to the object of anger. When we're howling abuse at someone because they have hurt us or taken us for granted we get some kind of tunnel vision of the senses. We don't hear, smell, touch or taste anything else – our sphere of thought is locked into this communication. In a certain sense we're living very much in the now and being quite present in our wrath. If we look at the Energy of anger in this way we can see in it all kinds of positive qualities, ones that in some ways it could be good to tune in to.

Because anger is a distorted form of Clarity it will obviously still display certain qualities of Clarity. We are not discussing two entirely different energies, because anger and Clarity are dynamically linked. We are not talking about polarities or opposites such as conveyed by the Taoist idea of Yin and Yang – that is a different kind of concept and a different way of looking at the world. We are talking about an Energy that has apparently become constricted. The Innate Primordial Wisdom of Clarity is the potential Energy of anger in the artificial condition of duality.

Anger arises when our reaction to the experience of Space is one of fear. We feel that we need to make instant reprisals the moment we become aware that someone could be taking advantage of us. We feel vulnerable, brittle and hollow sometimes – as if we were a thin sheet of ice on a pond ready to crack at the slightest pressure. This feeling gives rise to aggression and intolerance as powerful forces within our persona. We hope that our display of hostility will deter anyone from using, abusing or humiliating us. Anger becomes our way of communicating with the world, our way of proving to ourselves and others that we are real. We feel ourselves to be fragile and exposed, as if we were on a knife edge. So, anyone who threatens us in any way has to be dealt with by means of instant reprisals. for a hand we'll take an arm and for an arm we'll hack off a head. It's all very barbaric in that way, and whether it's the barbarism of an ancient war-lord or the sophisticated barbarism of boardroom power play makes little difference.

When the Energy of anger is functioning in its characteristic way, even the most dull and witless amongst us will suddenly find themselves equipped with unfamiliar skills. We develop an incredible memory and seem to be able to dredge up all manner of pertinent past events at the drop of a hat that are guaranteed to cut the subject of our anger to the quick. We seem to be able to choose just the right words with unprecedented wit and sarcasm. We parry the remarks of the other person with the lightning speed of a Samurai – every comment can be a rapier thrust that penetrates some vital organ. The more we develop our intellectual faculties, the more we are able to hone the cutting edge of our rage. But inevitably we run out of words, and when words fail the Energy carries through into physical violence. Anger and aggression are symptomatic of our feelings of weakness and fear. When we resort to anger we are saying that we are afraid – we are saying that we are too timid to express how we feel with honesty.

We only get angry if we feel that the other person is stronger than us in some way. This may be a little hard to understand especially for battered wives, but strength is perceived in many different ways and just because we are able to beat someone up does not mean that we feel that we are stronger. There is emotional strength, intelligent strength, moral strength, the strength that radiates from security and the strength of conviction or faith. Physical strength and verbal aggression tend to be overt and generally non-enduring, whereas the more abstract strengths tend to be covert and enduring. So, anger arises when we are confronted with people's strength that we seem to find lacking in ourselves. We are afraid that they will have all the answers. We feel that it could be useless to discuss the matter calmly because if we did we would have to expose our feelings of insecurity. We couldn't possibly admit our fears because actually we're quite embarrassed about them – they don't quite match up to our cherished intellectual prowess or the dogged stamina of our bloody-mindedness. We feel that we would be laughed at if we expressed weakness, so rather than face the possibility of gaining disrespect we latch onto the idea that attack is the best form of defence.

If our aggressive intellectual assault is pulled apart by our opponent and we are shown up as being unreasonable, misguided, self-seeking or generally reprehensible in some way then a punch in the mouth seems to be the last resort. Sadly the punch in the mouth is the first step along the road to atomic weapons, so we need to be careful that we don't labour under the misapprehension that wars are created by evil power-mongers who are so very different from us. Looked at in that way either they don't seem to be so bad or we don't seem to be so good.

We cannot seem to recognise that our only real strength lies in acknowledging our weakness – our weakness only exists as such because we keep it locked in some sort of emotional high security vault.

This could give us a whole new perspective on our anger and on the anger that is projected at us by others. The idea that angry people feel weak and fearful may seem to be a total contradiction because that is just the way we feel when we are having the anger projected at us. We feel this way because we look at what is happening only at a surface level. It would seem quite bizarre to us that we were having to endure the projection of this anger because someone feared our strength. If we were to realise that often anger is only projected at us because we seem to be strong we might be able to be gentle with the angry person. If instead of protecting ourselves from the anger we were able to recognise our own strength as the latent ability to expose our own feelings of vulnerability, we might find that angry people became unable to maintain their anger. If in the midst of our anger we could grasp the notion that we are afraid, we may be able to discover sufficient reserves of courage to make that admission to the other person. Having self-disclosed in this way we may well find that we are reassured by the other person that our feelings of insecurity and inadequacy are groundless. Usually we are so afraid of self-disclosure that the 'anger/attack' and 'assault/defence' habits repeat themselves throughout our lives.

As a transmuted Energy, anger is Mirror-Wisdom – Undistracted, Undistorted Clarity. But in order for us to find this Clarity or polish this mirror, we need to cut the insidious process of justification. Justification is the authority we invoke to license our anger – so it is important that we should not allow ourselves the misguided indulgence of justification. This is not so easy (to put it mildly!) because the process of justification is a strong part of our education and a salient feature of the world's cultural heritage. The nuclear balance of terror is part of that process, the spectrum of communist to fascist politics is part of that process, and unfortunately it has also become part of the very ideologies that have arisen to benefit humanity. How often have we heard ourselves saying, "Of course I'm bloody well angry – wouldn't anyone be!" The concept that we have every right to feel anything we feel needs to be called seriously into question. We might say that these negative emotions are 'only natural' but what does that actually mean? We can feel hot, we can feel cold, we can feel hunger, thirst or physical pain, but the realm of our emotions is not so easily defined because emotional responses differ from person to person. The emotions fall into an entirely different category – feeling cold is devoid of concept. Concepts may arise from our feeling cold but were the concepts to disappear the coldness would remain. But what of the emotions, what remains of them when the concepts disappear? This is what we are looking at when we practise Shi-ne. This is what we are looking at in order that we can grow and rediscover our Authentic Nature. What is natural for a human being to feel? Were any of us issued with the official handbook at birth? We could say that loneliness was natural if we are deprived of company, but there are hermits in all cultures who don't fit in with that idea, and they are certainly not all misanthropes. There are of course misanthropes and also loners, people who actively like to go off on their own, people who feel crowded in by others and who will soon remind you that they need their space if you impinge on them too much. Such people are not just exceptions to the rule that we need company. If we look at any aspect of our lives we can always find people who don't seem to share our needs. We can also be aware that other people seem to have needs that we don't share.

All this doesn't add up to an argument in favour of imposing some regime of mortification on ourselves. The Mystic Path does not compulsorily require that we ignore every emotional need. We can respect our own unique pattern of Energy and learn to work with it in a harmonious way. We can develop some sort of recognition of how we are tied by our emotional needs and how our emotional needs create life crises when they conflict with *what is*. It is a delicate balance and one that requires the experience of Space so that we don't indulge ourselves or brutalise ourselves. The experience of Intrinsic Space in this sense helps us to View our emotions with a touch of humour – with more sanity and real perspective.

So, fundamentally we're left with the View that it is not possible to say: "You have made me angry!" All we can say is: "I have made myself angry in reaction to what I have perceived you to have done to me." In that way we make ourselves completely responsible for what we feel – we stop laying the responsibility on other people. Taking responsibility for whatever it is that we may happen to be feeling is what enables us to kill justification.

Like the Sky Dancers, there are other anthropomorphic symbols of our Enlightened Consciousness in the Tibetan Tantric traditions and some appear as terrifying Beings. Ekajati, the 'Single-plait Mother' grasps a ripped-out heart in her hand which symbolises that justification should be uncompassionately murdered. Spilling the heart-blood of justification allows us to be *gentle people*. We become more relaxed and able to discover ourselves. The Intrinsic Space of our Beginninglessness generates Compassion for others.

This does not add up to letting people walk all over us – taking responsibility for how we are feeling means that we can be clear about how we respond. We do not need anger to help us right the wrongs of the world – we can work for peace, equality, harmony just as determinedly without it. If there is injustice in the world or in our personal situation our anger doesn't help, it just gets in the way. With the discovery of Space we find ourselves responding Openly about how we feel. The Mystic Path does not inhibit us from taking action based on our heart-intelligence – if we allow people to destroy us or our shared environment we are certainly not doing them any favours.

So, in our practice of working with anger, we need to rely more on our own Intrinsic Space than on neurotic thought processes and habitual responses. Negative emotions are maintained by the process of thinking about them rather than experiencing them at the non-conceptual level. The only way out is to let our Awareness rest with whatever emotion has arisen and experience it purely.

When we let go of justification we are no longer so much involved with maintaining the integrity of our self-image and the Energy of anger is no longer coloured or diffused by our need to prove that we exist through aggression.

When the 'subject–object dichotomy' dissolves into Space, anger can no longer exist as anger but as total Clarity which dispassionately reflects all that it sees. Nothing is left out, nothing is added – we see the whole picture in all its vibrant detail.

This Unconditioned Clarity is displayed by the brilliance, clearness and calmness of Water. The undisturbed surface of Water mirrors the sky perfectly and has the crystal Clarity which seems incapable of bias or distortion. When water is clear it is barely visible apart from the dimensionless brilliant reflective quality of its surface. We can see the pebbles, shingle, stones, rocks, weeds and fish as if there were no Water present.

This pure and undistorting Reflective Quality is symbolised by the 'Me-long' or 'Magic Mirror of Mind'. The Me-long is a very special symbol in Tibetan Tantra because it displays the Intrinsic Quality of Mind in terms of its Innate Reflective Capacity. In the Teaching of Dzogchen there are three Methods of Transmitting Teachings: Oral, Symbolic and Direct. The Me-long is used in the Symbolic Transmission. The Oral Transmission consists of the verbal or 'whispered' instruction that a Lama gives to an apprentice. The Symbolic Transmission consists of the Lama showing a symbol such as the Me-long or a crystal in order to convey meaning at a less conceptual level. Direct Transmission consists of Mind to Mind communication which is entirely free of concept. The Me-long which is a circular mirror usually made of silver or brass is used a great deal in the Symbolic Transmission and conveys a very important Teaching on the Nature of Mind. This is something of the explanation that accompanies the Me-long or Mirror. Although the Mirror has reflections they are not and do not define the Mirror – they only exist because the Mirror has the capacity to reflect. But although the reflections are not the Mirror, they cannot be divided from the Mirror – we only see the Mirror by virtue of the presence of the reflections. We define the Mirror as being the reflections we see in it, and rarely glimpse the Empty Mirror – the fundamental Creative Capacity. We see the Mirror because of the reflections in it and whether the reflections are beautiful or ugly the Mirror itself is unperturbed – it reflects everything equally and accurately. This explanation of Mind grows in meaning as our practice of Shi-ne develops and becomes profound. In the Awareness-imagery of Tibet the Me-long is sometimes seen hanging on the chests of Great Masters of the Dzogchen Lineage (Great Completeness). The Master Azom Drugpa, the previous incarnation of Lama Namkhai Norbu Rinpoche, is often depicted in this way in paintings.

Water can have the crispness and the sharpness of ice, with no blurred edges, no areas of confusion. Nothing is indistinct, hazy or difficult to discern. The landscape glitters with the patterns of frozen Water.

The cardinal direction traditionally associated with the field of Energy of the White Sky Dancer is the East where the Sun rises and which streams with the cool dispassionate light of Dawn.

The formalised Tibetan symbol for this Energy-field is the Dorje, the Thunderbolt Wand. The Dorje is said to have qualities of sharpness, total precision and Absolute Indestructibility. It is immovable, which is to say that it is undistractable and devoid of inherent tendencies. It is also known as the Adamite or Diamond Wand because it is the hardest substance and as such it is able to cut through everything without itself being cut. It is Completely and Directly incisive.

The season associated with this Energy-field is Winter, and the landscape is pristine and clear-cut. The snow has made drift-ridges that curve with beautiful precision. The white hills in the distance hold no secrets – the landscape is Open and devoid of confusion. Sounds carry in the clear cold air and find no surfaces from which to bounce distorted echoes. There is an enormous sense of tranquillity, there is the purity of silently falling snow and the sparkling geometry of crystalline structures.

Red – Mar (dMar)

9
The Energy Field
of the Red Sky Dancer

The colour red is connected to the Element of Fire, to the distorted energy of grasping and the Liberated Energy of Discriminating Awareness.

Fire is a vital passionate force that devours its world – it can be omniverous, consuming everything with which it makes contact. Fire is a sensuous Energy – we speak of our ardour being kindled, of our burning with passion and of our flames of desire. Popular love songs often have lines about setting the night on fire or setting each other on fire. Sexual arousal is often spoken of in strictly inflammatory terms. Poetry has always explored the different forms of combustion to describe passion from sparks and embers to conflagrations. We talk about 'having the hots' for somebody, and if it fizzles out or if we are left broken-hearted we feel cold and our vision projects coldness onto our world. These aspects of our language are by no means accidental or coincidental – we are actually always in touch with the Empty Essence of our Elements because our enlightenment is always present but unmanifested.

The ravenous need to possess is choiceless; it leaves us no room to observe ourselves. Because we cannot allow any distance to arise between us and the objects of our desire there is no perspective and no room for our discriminatory faculties to function. There is no room for us to appreciate the objects of our desire because we are fettered by the intense claustrophobia of the process of grasping. We throw ourselves into life and invariably miss – we get too drunk, stay up too late, go to too many parties, get off on too many highs and attempt to squeeze every last drop of pleasure out of everything. Over indulgence becomes a way of life and we become dissatisfied with anything simple and

unmixed. We like multi-media entertainment: we like to be talking to a friend, glancing at a picture book whilst the stereo is on.
We like the television to be on too, but with the sound off; we like
to have a cigarette in one hand and a cup of coffee in the other. We
overdo everything and burn ourselves out in the process.

We want to escalate everything. We think, "Wouldn't it be
great to make love to the most beautiful person in the world!"
We'd have wild synthesised sounds playing and we'd have some
very fine old Calvados brandy. There'd be soft, beautiful lighting
– no, even better, we'd have a strobe, a red one, and the ceiling
above the bed would have a large mirror on it. In fact there'd be
mirrors all over the place and a video camera relaying every
moment on a screen somewhere else. But we think of something
better again. We'd be wrapped in our passionate embrace free-
falling from an aircraft over the Sahara and we'd land in the most
fabulous oasis with a refrigeration plant full of ice-cold coconut
rum and freshly crushed orange juice. There'd be the sound of
frenzied arabesque zither music in the air and from the heat haze
over the dunes mirages of everything you could ever imagine
would be dissolving in and out of each other, lyrically incandesc-
ing with the fluttering wings of the music. Unfortunately it's just
very sad. It's all a day dream that actually denigrates our lives and
the person we may be relating to because we're never content to
appreciate the amazing qualities of what is actually unfolding
around us Here and Now. There's nothing right or wrong, good
or bad about our dream, but we're not actually doing it. And if we
prefer our dream to what is actually going on, our relationship
with our situation and those with whom we communicate, then
it's rather insulting and degraded.

Fire exhibits the quality of desire and at the same time the quality of objects of desire. Fire is provocative, seductive and flirta-
tious – we sometimes illustrate the lascivious quality of Fire when
we speak of logs in a fire being licked by the flames. Fire displays
glamour, tinsel and surface attraction – it's the fireworks of life, a
magnificent pryotechnic performance.

Fire, however, can warm us, serving our needs as a centre or focal point of comfort and sustenance. It maintains our bodily temperature when otherwise it would be too cold to survive. The startling bright forks of its flames keep away the predatory beasts of the night and give us a sense of being protected. We use it to cook our food and its heat brings out the subtle flavours of our ingredients that blend together harmoniously to furnish us with food to enjoy. We use it to fashion our metal implements and to harden the clay of our drinking vessels. Its incandescence illuminates the darkness enabling us to read or carry on other activities when the light of the sun has gone. Its visual excitement and cheering crackle stimulates us and puts us at our ease. It's a source of comfort and well-being which enables us to be merry. We can sit and gaze for hours at its hypnotic transmogrifying forms, intrigued, delighted and fascinated.

Fire is a Shamanic art and lighting a good fire in the open air with flint and tinder can take the Fire-maker closer to the Fire Element: a relationship is developed. We could discover that we are surrounded by Fire – the Fire of the sun, moon and stars; the Fire of angler fish, glow-worms, fireflies, fox-fire and the Northern Lights; the Fire of our interaction with our world and our Fire of enthusiasm – our 'Good Heart' that extends itself to others. But Fire needs to be respected because it can get out of control, our desires need to be experienced with a certain lightness otherwise they stick like napalm.

We need to learn the Art of Dream-like window shopping a little, to learn to admire and enjoy the passing display of phenomena without feeling the need to grab at them. I remember once when I had just returned from my first trip to the Himalayas and was visiting a friend. We were sitting in the garden sipping orange-juice and exchanging stories when he said how nice it would be if we could get out into the country for the day. We were in the garden of a house owned by the university where my friend was a student, and being overheard by a friend who wasn't using his car that day, the keys were tossed over to us in jaunty style with the words, "Pour in some juice and take a ride." The car was a ginchy little number, a red two-seater with a walnut facia and an in-flight stereo. Off we went down the road and thoroughly enjoyed every moment of it. It was a splendid day and we'd made up a very pleasant hamper with a flask of real coffee and a bottle of chilled wine in a thermo-bag. When we got back and were sitting comfortably in his room, I couldn't help noticing that my friend was very quiet. Usually he's a talkative young man so before long it became obvious to me that something was amiss. I asked him what was wrong. He shrugged my question off a few times but finally admitted that not having a car like the one we'd spent the day in had really got to him. It's a dangerous business playing with Fire or desire unless you have some experience of Intrinsic Space.

This is not to say that we should avert our gaze from all objects that are attractive to us, refusing to acknowledge the beauty or value of anything that is not ours. Neither is it to say that we should only taste or experience what can be ours. Nothing can be ours forever even if we are able to obtain it. This doesn't mean total renunciation of the world, but that we should try to develop our View a little so that with the experience of Intrinsic Space which we discover through the practice of Shi-ne; humour develops in the fabric of our perception. We need to be able to touch, hear, see, smell and taste – to really appreciate, but then to be able to really let go.

There is a story of two monks who came upon a very dignified lady on the bank of a wide but fairly shallow river that they were used to wading across. The lady was dressed up in all her finery for the very special occasion of the wedding of her friend in the next village. She too was fairly used to wading across but on this particular day she was worried about the possibility of losing her footing and having to arrive at the wedding drenched. One of the monks offers to carry her across and picking her up in his arms wades across to the other side. The two monks accompany the lady a mile or two along the path until she turns off into the village where her friend's wedding is taking place. As the two monks carry on their way one of them is very obviously pondering serious issues and finally he has to make his thoughts known to his companion: "Do you think it prudent for us monks to have such close contact with ladies?" The older monk lets out a great laugh and says, "I put the lady down back at the river but it looks like you're still carrying her."

The distorted energy of the Fire Element might seem very similar in some ways to the materialism of the Earth Element. But whereas the distorted Earth Element acquires and hoards without any real joy in possession, the distorted Fire Element energy consumes and discards with a certain fevered glee. With Earth it's more important to solidify ourselves with immense quality and quantity so that we feel strong and impervious, but with Fire we find our moment of security in the moment of consumption. Once we have got what it was that we thought we wanted it is fairly swiftly neglected.

Our confrontation with our Intrinsic Space has been one that we fear as exposing us to our isolation. We feel very much alone in the world and need to possess and be possessed to cover over our feelings of isolation. The act of anticipating impending ownership, of planning how we'll get what we want is a crucial part of our energy – we approach our relationships with people in the same crude sort of way. We live for the moment when we pass the readies over the counter and exultantly caress the new record, the new car, the new whatever. This is an external approximation of the extermination of isolation we wish to achieve through ecstatic union with the object of our desire. But no matter how often we consummate our desire we find ourselves unable to fill our emptiness. We cannot appease the threat of Intrinsic Space in that way, because we could pour the entire phenomenal world into it and it would just vanish. We need to look into our desire at a non-conceptual level and Liberate its Boundless Energy.

The distorted energy of Fire depersonalises our relationship with everything. We are unable to relate properly to anyone else because we are always using them to obliterate our terrible loneliness and isolation. We want everybody to like us; we want our partners to love us more than their own lives. We are so clinging and possessive that we are always demanding new signs of loyalty and questioning the limits of their love and commitment. If we make a new friend we tend to go round too often, crowding their lives with our presence and wearing out our welcome. We ask too much of people – sometimes we can be very generous but it is not real generosity, only our desire to buy people's friendship so that we will never ever have to be alone.

The Liberated field of Energy of the Fire Element displays the discriminative quality of Fire which is realised in terms of how it helps us in specific ways. The oxyacetaline torches of workers in precious metals enable them to direct fine points of flame to the exact point required. In the field of medicine the laser-beam is used in micro-surgery achieving incredible precision in the art of healing.

Once we gain some recognition of Intrinsic Space we discover that our loneliness is actually *aloneness* which is a positive, uninhibited, unattached *frame of non-reference*. We no longer burn with the need to grasp and possess for ourselves alone – our entire fabric of experience becomes more spacious. We Centre on the isolation, vulnerability and insecurity of others – the Fire of passion become the *passion beyond passion* which we could call 'Compassion' or Pure Appropriateness. Indiscriminate grasping is Liberated into the pure Energy-field of Discriminating Awareness.

As soon as we cease to operate from the 'centralised-desire-fulfilment-machine' of distracted-being we extend ourselves infinitely to all Beings. We are immediately Aware of exactly what is needed and where it is needed. When people come to us with their problems we don't have to use that situation to make ourselves feel wanted. We don't have to make people dependent upon us but can facilitate their self-discovery in a skilful way. We don't give too little or too much because we are not governed by our own fears and anxieties. There is a distinct difference between the *real compassion* of Pure Appropriateness and the 'idiot compassion' that helps little old persons across the street whether they want to go or not.

Discriminative Awareness means Being in tune, Being able to listen without the babbling of our internal gossip getting in the way.

Having realised that we don't have to consume anything in order to establish our existence we realise that we already possess everything. Our every activity is the consummation of our 'love-affair' with Emptiness and phenomena. We are free of reference-points as objects of desire, so Space becomes Open to us and we can enjoy the spontaneity of its Play without feeling isolated. We burn with the Wisdom-Fire of Centrelessness and Realise our Capacity to Extend our Realisation to Everyone.

The formalised Tibetan symbol for this field of Energy is Pema, the Lotus. The Lotus is an important symbol in the Tibetan Tantric systems and all Awareness-Beings used in the practice of Visualisation are described as sitting on Lotus-thrones. Padmasambhava whose name means 'Lotus-Born' crystallised the essence of this symbol in His Being and in His Life which continues through His Deathlessness in the Energy of His Accomplished Lineage.

The symbolism of the Lotus is that it grows up out of the dark mud and slime of polluted water into dazzling sunlight. When it Opens, its petals are Pristine and unaffected by the mire. Its petals have been pure from Beginninglessness and remain pure through the illusion of its renunciation of apparent darkness and its Transmutation into Clear Light.

The colour Red is a warm cosy glow, it reminds us of youthful rosy cheeks and all the vibrant, vigorous aspects of life. It can also be 'painting the town red' in a desperate attempt to mask our isolation.

The cardinal direction of this field of Energy is the West where the Sun sets with the scenic grandeur of its polychromatic festival of light. We could be in some tranquil place of natural beauty – soft green cliff tops may have provided a comfortable place for us to sit with our backs against a rock warmed by the day's sunshine. The sea is lapping on miles of fine golden sand filigreed by coves and large free-standing columns of rock that have the simple perfection of a Japanese rock garden. The cry of seagulls descants the rippling sea and there is a soothing breeze fresh from the sea that eases the heat of the day – it invigorates us. We feel alive, scintillated and relaxed – there is a feeling that everything is just as it should be. There are many little flowers that scent the breeze and densely packed camomile cushions the place where we sit. The sun becomes a brilliant deep red – a translucent disc of light that scatters reflections on the numberless waves that sparkle and glitter for our enrapturement. The colours all around us are soft and velvety – we luxuriate in the completely accommodating simplicity of our surroundings. We feel young, healthy and expansive – the vastness of the coloured sky is Open to us.

There is the wish to share the delightful efflorescence of this scene with others. There is no thought of wanting to witness this brilliant display on our own – the performance is so lyrical. The concept of being a privileged one-member audience has no appeal at all. The idea does not even occur to us because this is something we naturally wish to share. It is appropriate that there should be a full house, not only for the sake of the actresses' (the Sky Dancers') efforts but for each member of the audience to celebrate their shared appreciation. Even if there is no one with us, our feelings of warmth and 'Good Heart' toward others extend beyond ourselves as a *natural reflex*.

This field of Energy is associated with the Spring, with freshness and vitality – the charming play of young creatures, the joy of being able to jump around and leap with excitement at any age. There is the wonder of impending growth; buds succulent with life decorate the bare branches of the trees and some are bursting into leaf and flower. There are catkins and bluebells in the woods, delicate green shoots sprouting into the light. The atmosphere is one of joyous frivolity and lightness. Cultivating *real frivolity* in our lives necessitates *cutting through seriousness*. We take ourselves so seriously that our spiritual quest becomes like too much porridge – we can't possibly eat all this awful stuff so it just hangs around in our minds getting older and harder until when offering it to our friends they damage their teeth on it. Some people become so serious that it seems as if they've been rolling around in porridge, their homes are full of it, they hang it on their walls, they fill their vocabulary with it and try to impregnate other

other people with it. Cutting through seriousness enables us to feel the sunshine and the fine nourishing rain that refreshes the world and fills the sky with Magical Rainbows.

Green – Jang (lJang)

10

The Energy Field
of the Green Sky Dancer

The colour Green is connected to the Element of Air, to the distorted energy of paranoia and the Liberated Energy of Self-fulfilling Activity.

Air flurries in all directions, touching everything, exploring every surface, examining every angle and investigating every crevice. It is almost as if it were always seeking but never finding – it has to press on, constantly searching and unable to rest. Air can be a breeze or a strong wind. It can be forceful and destructive like a hurricane which destroys the obstacles in its path.

The circling energy of a whirlwind sums up the qualities of paranoia – it's an energy that continually chases its tail leaving havoc in its wake in the same way that we lash out and drag other people into our own paranoia. In the circularity of this energy we impel ourselves to go over the same ground over and over again. We're going off on holiday and we've lost our passport so we look through the same drawer three or four times before finding it there.

The distorted energy of the Air Element is fundamentally concerned with 'losing ground'. We validate our existence in terms of territory. We feel that we have some sort of territory that is under attack and we feel that we need to engage in a constant hot and cold war in its defence. Our reaction to confronting our Intrinsic Space has manifested as fear of obliteration. We feel that Space has such a deadly finality about it that it has the power to squeeze us into utter annihilation. We fear Space as a militant nihilistic force – like some 'grim reaper' with a horrible bony golf club who wants to putt us into a 'black hole'. Space means death to us and death seems to mean the big full stop in the sky. This concept develops into a hyperactive kind of cowardice in which we fear any hint of sensory deprivation. In the Visionary world we are afraid of darkness. In the Auditory world we are afraid of silence. In the Sensory fields we fear loss of territory.

This field of Energy has certain similarities with the feeling of isolation of the Fire Element, but there is a significant difference. With the Fire Element, we feel that we have no territory – we identify ourselves in terms of our isolation. With the Air Element we identify ourselves in terms of territory so that if our territory ceased to exist we would also cease to exist. We feel that we could be crushed into nothing and so rather than being concerned with grasping we are concerned with trying to maintain what we have and what we feel that we are.

We see ourselves as under threat. There seems to be some sort of conspiracy both inherent in the world and contrived by parties known and unknown to undermine or obliterate us. Our mode of existence has become a self-protecting mechanism. We have projected our sense of personality beyond ourselves and any encroachment on our territory such as our football team or political party being vilified, is felt as a personal blow. No one can disagree with anything we say without it feeling like a major assault on us. The use of the word 'territory' is both physical and psychological and refers to an inability to distinguish the abstract from the concrete. In extreme cases we might be severely threatened if someone told us that they didn't like our favourite colour.

The threats that seem to come at us from all angles keep us always on our toes – we are very edgy indeed. We feel the need to be on our guard – we have to generate constant vigilance against suspected adversaries who are hatching plots for our downfall. There seems to be something about the world that we never quite seem to get taped up. There's obviously something crucial going on that we find ourselves unable to get in on. People have secrets that they're not sharing and give each other knowing glances when they think that we're not looking. If we catch them at it they turn and smile at us which is infuriating. They're so confident that they don't even seem to care that we're on to them. All those people out there are so completely solid and assured and we feel so open to attack. We suspect even people who are close to us – do they know we know or do they guess? Do they know that we know that they know, or do they suspect? When we're talking to people we somehow know that they're not saying quite what they mean and that they have some kind of information that they've not going to impart to us. We ask questions but we get no answers, or if we do they are answers that are couched in such a way as to harbour a multiplicity of interpretations. We see ambiguities in harmless comments when people have just called round to say hello. We pump our friends for answers to what is being said about us and when we get no response we believe there is something sinister going on and they want to keep us in the dark.

We become highly sophisticated in our encyclopedic analysis, we dissect every word, nuance and gesture as conveying some meaning that we need to take into our calculations. We become ridiculously nimble, preposterously alert – we are ready at any moment to repel invaders. But this acute alertness of ours is really only a state of tension, a state of agitation – we have become the complete psychotic athlete.

We are jealous of the seeming security of the people around us. We envy their sophisticated security systems which enable them to operate with such ease and confidence. We think that if only we could find the secret to that kind of security that we'd 'be there' as well. But it's not possible – the secret is closely guarded and probably everyone is part of the plain-clothes security network that is keeping tabs on us.

We invest all our energy in trying to fathom the motivations of those around us. We're suspicious of them and wonder why they're trying to befriend us. Maybe they're trying to lure us into a sense of false security in order to take advantage of us, undermine our identity or steal our ideas. We wonder why they seem to want to help us – there must be some kind of ulterior motive, some conspiracy. We burn up our physical and mental resources trying to fathom it all out but we arrive at no firm conclusions just more questions. We have become characters from the world of Franz Kafka. In 1984, the year made vaguely infamous by George Orwell, I saw an interesting badge which read: "Even if you're not paranoid it doesn't mean that they're not out to get you!" Now at this point I really wouldn't like anyone to get the idea that the Mystic Path implies some sort of ostrich-like naivety as the goal. If we become completely unsuspecting all it means is that we have lost contact with the reality of the world around us and are living, or attempting to live, with our faculties swaddled in candy-floss. We need to Observe the sensation of paranoia in the moment Now, because, after all, the condition of feeling paranoid doesn't in itself protect us from those who *are* out to get us.

Our energies are randomly scattered and so we have little capacity for the fulfilment of our Natural Creativity. We are unable to enhance our lives or those of others because we burn up all our energies in the maintenance of territory and in the protection of our 'street-image'. We wear ourselves out with our relentless thinking, which ironically only tightens our nervousness through increasing our feelings of vulnerability. Paranoia is a 'self-fulfilling energy'. We think that no one likes us to visit and so we act in such a way when we are asked to visit as to guarantee that a date never gets fixed. After a while no one asks us to visit any more which gives us something real to get paranoid about. This self-fulfilment quality of paranoia adds weight to our belief in the accuracy of our fears and the whole process escalates to absurd proportions.

With our energy in this confused state there is no possibility of harnessing our potential. We cannot even explore any supposed threat properly because we are always having to divide our attention between all the other threats and the new threats that seem to be constantly arising. We live in panic that we are going to be caught off guard at any moment, that our electricity or telephone may be cut off, or that someone will find out about the night we did whatever it was. We get gripped by anxiety and tension –

we're as taut as bow strings waiting to release arrows of self-protective impulse. But our concentration is split and our arrows always miss the mark or we muff it altogether – the arrow slips and rips out our thumbnail.

This is obviously extreme. The character of this Energy-field can cover the spectrum from being a worrier to being a paranoid-schizophrenic. This energy can manifest in a great variety of ways according to the balance of our other energies. In the 'spiritual world' we are always flitting from one teacher to another, comparing and contrasting but never actually practising. First we have to find what we imagine is going to be totally right for us, as it has to meet our strict intellectual approval. So we are constantly asking questions and arguing with the answers. The questions we ask have little or nothing to do with Real Experience, but are based solely on our whirlpool intellect. Our intellect generates such a pervasive charge that what we take to be our emotions are virtually just reverberations of our despotic rationality. This means that when we say we are expressing our feeling all we are often doing is describing how we are churning up our emotional being with the process of intellect. We become very confused and unable to settle. We are unable to trust anyone else, so it becomes very difficult for us to actually trust ourselves enough to develop any Real Commitment to a Path.

The Liberated field of Energy of the Air Element is the strong steady wind that enables ships to make good headway rather than the tornado that wrecks them. It is the fresh clean wind in our hair that enables us to shake off our lethargy – we have the feeling that we could accomplish anything. The discovery of Intrinsic Space enables us to let go of our anxieties which dissipate into Emptiness. We Realise that the ground of our suspicion and worry is nonexistent. It dawns on us that our paranoia, the vicious circle of our intellect, was just our way of trying to prevent ourselves from vanishing. When we gain some degree of Clarity we View *vanishing* as an occupational *hazard* of being – we continually *vanish* and continually *reappear*. We are continually leaping out of sheer Emptiness into the moment Now.

I remember the intense anxiety I felt when I first dived into the sea from a low cliff edge. I'd been watching someone diving off the cliff for a while from where I'd been dozing on the beach and it had seemed like a good idea to me. I took a walk over, but when I got there I thought: "No way am I going to dive off here!" I could see the pale green rocks below the surface of the water and realised that I'd actually have to dive outwards a little. I physically squirmed at the thought of my possible impact with those barnacle-encrusted serpentine rocks. Even if it were possible for me I might louse up and snag my foot on something and slither over the edge. It was a problem, because I really wanted to make that dive – I really wanted to be the sort of person who did that sort of thing. I spent a while thinking myself into a state of intractable incapacity but was interrupted when I noticed some ladybirds, unusual ones I'd not seen before. There was a yellow one, a few small orange ones and an enormous red one. I watched the big red one for a while and completely forgot about the dive and the possibility of the gory bits of me left pink and grisly on the rocks when the lifeguards had taken me away. The big red one was pigging-out on green aphids and it was fascinating to watch its movements. Finally it flew away so I got up, took a good long run and sailed off the cliff edge. Suddenly I was in the water plummeting down, turning slowly and rising again to the surface. The top of my head tingled a bit but it felt amazing – I was full of wordless gratitude for whatever it was that had enabled me to make that dive. The *whatever*, was the Space I'd experienced observing the tiny movements of the ladybird and the decision to dive was the first idea that sprang from that Space. If I'd questioned it I would have had to have walked back to the beach, but as it was I swam.

Learning to trust Intrinsic Space, the Space between 'known' areas of experience, is the Basis of Growth – without it we stagnate. We have to have some kind of trust that we will wake up again every time we go to sleep. Trust is vital, and trusting in the Spaciousness of our True Nature is imperative in the process of letting go of paranoia. As soon as our paranoia dissolves into

Intrinsic Space our Energy is released and able to Flow Freely.

Being able to Act directly without inhibition is a quality of the Realisation of Intrinsic Space. We can move with Complete Commitment in any direction without having to concern ourselves with the dubious benefits of military tactics. There is no need to trouble ourselves with the ins and outs of rearguard action because there are no supply lines to protect. We are not in hostile territory so our troops have no need of rations and ammunition – they're all quite merrily enjoying the countryside anyway. We're no longer concerned with launching offensives and consolidating our defences because no one is pitting themselves against us. What we thought were the enemy are just other people not so very different from ourselves – maybe they had different ideas, sang different songs, ate different food or spoke differently. We discover that in some ways the world is a little kinder than we'd previously imagined. We discover that not only is the earth a kinder place but that what conflicts there are, are an aspect of the way that people react to each other's pain.

Loss of paranoia is one hell of a big relief. There are no more strategies to be worked out – no more suspicion of mutiny in the ranks and no more war. We are not stifled by paranoia, there is nothing left to keep under surveillance and our need of territory to protect ourselves from annihilation evaporates. There is nothing to guard and no permanent, separate, solid or continuous 'I' to be guarded anyway.

We have the Wisdom of Self-fulfilling Activity and are Free of all hindrances. We can Pacify what needs to be Pacified, we can Enrich what needs to be Enriched, we can Control what needs to be Controlled and we can Destroy what needs to be Destroyed. These are the four principles known as the Wisdom-Activity of the Sky Dancers – the Energetic Aspect of Enlightenment. Our Actions Fulfil themselves because we don't embark on projects founded on the viewpoint of distracted-being. Our Activities are Pure Appropriateness and their success/completion is implicit in their inception.

The Activities that spring Spontaneously from this Wisdom-

Energy are not always easily understood from the 'conditioned perspective'. In terms of Enlightened Activity we could be destroying a cherished belief which gave a believing aspirant some kind of inspiration. We could be enriching a quality in someone that they felt was irrelevant to their Spiritual growth. But this is not an 'ordinary perspective' and can only be comprehended from the Realisation of Intrinsic Space, in which all Activity is Present, Direct and Self-fulfilling.

Drukpa Kunley, the famous Tibetan Crazy-Wisdom Master, was a wandering Ngakpa renowned both for his Enlightenment and for his extraordinarily outrageous behaviour. In one story told of him, he came running into a village where a certain Geshe was giving a discourse on Logic. (The title 'Geshe' is like some sort of super-doctorate awarded to those monks who have spent many years in academic study of morality, philosophy and psychology. Only once they have been rigorously examined over days of long, gruelling debate are they given this recognition, and so naturally they are highly respected in the monastic traditions of Tibet.) Drukpa Kunley, accompanied as ever by his dog, was in hot pursuit of a deer which he slew with an arrow from his hunting bow right in front of the Teaching area – a great canopy of cloth rigged up like an open-sided tent in front of the monastery. Drukpa Kunley swiftly skinned the deer, spit-roasted it and feasted on the flesh leaving the rest for his dog. He washed it back with a flask of chang (the Tibetan barley beer he often drank) and leant back to rest in the sunshine. When the Geshe had finished his Teaching Drukpa Kunley let out a resonant belch and smiled at the angry monks who were approaching him. The assembly of monks was horrified and demanded in aggressive voices what right he had to disturb their important study with this cruel display. Drukpa Kunley told them with a grin that he had come to show them the fruition of what they were trying to learn, at which he threw the skin of the deer back over its neatly arranged bones and with a click of his fingers the deer sprang up as if nothing had happened and vanished into the woods.

He then pointed out that scholarship was one thing, but that

Knowing the Nature of Mind was another. The monks were fairly dumbfounded, not only by what they had seen and heard of Drukpa Kunley, but by the fact that the Great Geshe was laughing as heartily as Drukpa Kunley himself. They were actually good friends and the Geshe expected his friend the Mad Ngakpa to turn up every once in a while and perform some such tricks. Drukpa Kunley spent most of his life knocking the establishment, but everywhere he went to rock the boat a little they remember him with reverence.

Crazy-Wisdom is associated with the Awareness-Being Dorje-Tröllo (Thunderbolt Loose-hanging Stomach) who rides the Sky-Tiger Ati-mueh, an Awareness-Being of the Bonpo tradition. Dorje-Tröllo embodies what are known in some traditions especially the Dzogchen tradition as the 'Three Terrible Oaths'. These are: Whatever is to happen – may it happen! Whichever way it goes – may it go that way! There is no purpose! This adds up to 'positively willing every situation to be exactly as it is'. This is a very advanced kind of attitude and one that most people cannot relate to easily, but it is a *Direction* and as such may give us some inspiration in our practice.

The Crazy-Wisdom Activity of any Teacher usually carries a powerful message for us if we are Open to perceiving it. There is a delightful story of Milarepa that I would like to recount, partly to illustrate this idea and partly because I love telling it. Milarepa was a Ngakpa who lived most of his life in the mountains of southern Tibet. He was the pupil of a farmer called Marpa who gave him his Heart-Instruction and sent him off to practise in the mountain solitudes. Marpa had also been a Ngakpa, a married Lama who had received his instruction in turn from the wandering Tantric Master Naropa. The story of Milarepa's Life is known even outside Tibet because he stands out as being one of Tibet's greatest Masters.

One day whilst Milarepa was sitting outside his meditation cave he was visited by his sister who had come from a long way off to bring him some food and various other comforts. But when she saw that her brother was naked she felt quite ashamed and told him off for not looking after himself properly and losing all sense of decency. She went away and bought a length of cloth so that he could cover himself with it. In a few days she returned with the cloth and gave it to her brother who agreed to cover up his offending parts. So the sister is pleased that her saintly brother will be suitably dressed when other patrons call to bring offerings and goes off to make a short pilgrimage in the locality before saying goodbye to her brother. But when she comes to say goodbye to Milarepa she is shocked even more by what he has done with the cloth. Literally every vaguely penis-shaped part of his body has been covered with a neatly sewn tube including his nose, and he is sitting there looking completely bizarre. She asks him to explain himself and of course he does, but his answer is as bizarre as his appearance. He explains that he thought that as she had objected to the open display of his genitals that she might also object to the sight of anything similar, so he had covered it all up: penis, fingers, toes and nose. At this point his sister broke down and wept begging his forgiveness. She had not realised that her brother was Completely Beyond involvement with the non-sense criteria of everyday life and that she had herself not really understood what the practice of the Mystic Path was all about. At that point Milarepa gave her a wonderful Teaching on the practice of Tumo (Mystic-Heart) and she went off into retreat herself to become an accomplished Repa. The word Repa means cotton wearer and the name is applied to those who are proficient in the practice of developing Tumo the Psychic-Heat that enables them to live in sub-zero temperatures either naked or wearing only thin white cotton. Most of Milarepa's famous pupils had the name Repa as part of their name. Gampopa his pupil who was the forefather of the Kagyudpa School was known as his Heart-son like the Sun and Rechungpa (Little Repa) was known as his Heart-son like the Moon.

The formalised Tibetan symbol for this field of Energy is the Thunderbolt Sword. It Displays Unconstrained Power, Direct and Unhindered Action. No one would ever question the ease and freedom of the movement of lightning. Lightning doesn't waver, it doesn't weigh up the pros and cons of the situation or get caught up in doubts about when it might be best to strike. It doesn't hesitate before it reaches the ground but moves with complete purpose charging the Air with electricity.

The colour Green is associated with jealousy, envy and suspicion, but also with the activity of growth.

The cardinal direction of this field of Energy is the North where the Elements interact in an extreme fashion. The North wind is the strongest wind and the weather conditions in the North are erratic and changeable.

This field of Energy is connected with the Summer when life is teeming. Wherever you look insect activity is frenetic. The grasses in the fields and meadows are crawling with many millions of miniscule creatures all engaged in prolific activity. Nothing is static or at rest, even the Air seems to buzz and shimmer with a heat haze. Bees are humming from flower to flower and tadpoles are becoming frogs and leaping off in search of flies to eat. There are sudden dramatic thunderstorms that die away as quickly as they begin.

Early night is the time of this Energy when the Sun has set and the Air is vibrating with the sound of grasshoppers and crickets. The rooks are coming home to roost in trees and the sound of their cawing carries a long way. They jostle each other for perching positions and flap their wings. More come late and have to try to find themselves some space on the branches – they dislodge others and they get dislodged themselves. There's a constant squabble going on that never seems to draw to an end.

This imagery displays a small fraction of the incredible dynamism of this field of Energy which in its True Nature is the Essence of Power.

Blue – Ngön (sNgon)

11

The Energy Field
of the Blue Sky Dancer

The colour Blue is connected to Space, to the distorted energy of indifference and oblivious torpor, and the Liberated Energy of Ubiquitous Intelligence and All-Encompassing Space.

Space is probably mostly understood as 'outer space', that endless realm out there full of an incalculable number of stars and planetary systems, meteor showers, attenuated gases and the fantastic whirling shapes of the spiral galaxies. This 'outer space' certainly holds us with a sense of awe – it's an exhilarating Open frontier of our world that is full of strange possibilities and which stretches into endlessness. This 'outer space', and the possibility of its exploration, has given birth to a plethora of science-fiction material in which writers have been able to stretch their imaginations and those of their readers. It's a world of time-travel, co-existent universes and confrontations with alien civilisations which have developed in many different ways in contrast with our earthly civilisations.

But 'space' somehow remind us of Death, and can be misconceived as vacuity or blankness – there is nothing there, nothing can happen and there is no one even to perceive that nothing is happening. We back off in sheer terror at the idea of that complete and utter absence of anything, and recoil into a cocoon of our own mental fabrication. I once saw a film poster bearing the fascinating caption: 'In space no one can hear you scream!' This fear is a distortion because we have only encountered the idea of Space, and our idea is a product of our neurosis. We have comforted ourselves by conceptualising the Free Open Dimension of Space into the graveless grave of nihilism. Having named Space as something we don't want to think about we lose touch with the

Open Dimension of our Being and fester in mediocrity. We are unable to relate to an absence of tangibility – it does not conform to any sort of logic and we need some method of feeling comfortable about it.

Although we talk about Space in terms of nothingness, Death and the end of everything, these terms are polarised. We fail to realise that Everything – *just as it is* – has Emptiness or Space as its Fundamental Nature. *Nothing* can't be separated from the concept of *Something*. The concept of *Death* can't be separated from the concept of *Birth*. *The end* can't be separated from *the beginning*. Even the *idea* of a vacuum (which as we know 'nature abhors') suggests *substance* to which it can be compared. The Vastness of Space Encompasses every polarity – it is the Womb of Potentiality.

Space doesn't constitute an Element as do Earth, Water, Fire and Air, because Space is the Beginningless/Endless Origin of the Elements. It is within Space that the Elements Perform as the Primal Play of Reality – the Dance of the five Khandros. Space Continually Creates and Reabsorbs these fields of Energy without effort. The four distorted fields of Energy operate as defence mechanisms of the 'oblivious torpor' which arises from conceptualising Space into a dull fog of nothingness. Conversely, the four Liberated Energies Arise Naturally as the Dynamic Functions of Ubiquitous Intelligence and Complete Openness.

The frame of reference in which Space is conceptualised as a distorted field of Energy is one that numbs everything into a deadly semi-conscious cosiness. We play 'blind, deaf and dumb' to experience. We feel that life is too much for us, that reality is too painful. The thought of all that wretched life going on out there is just too much for us, so we're not going to play – we're going to creep off into a corner somewhere and forget about it in the fond hope that it's all conveniently going to slip away. We've come to the conclusion that we're not even going to think about the possibility of working with it or attempting to handle it. Everything has become far too much effort for far too little reward – when we're at our worst we feel hollow and worthless – our living space becomes a health hazard. We lie in bed most of the day, occasionally getting up to make a cup of tea or if we're pushed we'll make a slice of toast and smear it haphazardly with what ever happens to be lying around in the kitchen. The crumbs drop all over the floor and we wipe our mouths on our dressing gown or on some article of clothing that we've left lying on the floor. The rubbish bin is stinking and stuffed to capacity – the dishes in the sink pile up until there's nothing left to use before we make the effort to wash up a few things. The bedroom is festooned with clothes that need to be washed but we'll only do something about it when the combined sock and underwear stench has become so untenably ghastly that we start gagging on it. We only do the basic minimum and gradually the quality of our lives gets eroded more and more until a further sense of depression and pointlessness sets in.

In other cases maybe, we don't get so socially incapacitated but we often feel that we'd like to get drunk, sit staring vacantly at the television and round it all off with 'downers' of some sort. The last thing we want to hear about is that there are methods through which we can Experience the Pure Undiluted Energy of Being. Instead we contrive what we consider to be palatable ways of dealing with the inner gnawing sensation and the pain of the desolation that we feel.

There are five ways of dealing with the pain of desolation which are related to the five distorted fields of Energy. There is *freezing* which is connected to the distorted Energy field of Water. There is *consolidating* which connects to Earth, *fantasising* to Fire, *anticipating* to Air, and *obliterating* to Space. Of these five the three most fundamental are *fantasising*, *freezing* and *obliterating* because they are linked directly to the three distracted tendencies – *attraction, aversion* and *indifference* – which we have previously discussed.

Fantasising as a process of dealing with the pain of desolation is one in which we cling to our pain because we are convinced that it's all we've got left. We feed on the Energy of our pain like some kind of masochistic vampire. We nurture our pain with great skill. We grasp at the intensity of our pain and envisage ourselves as some sort of anti-hero or maybe some character in a Shakespearian tragedy. This is maybe a little in keeping with the western concept of the suffering artist. We fondly imagine that great things might come out of our agony. I'm sure that some people will want to argue this point because a great deal of our artistic heritage has been inspired within the context of human suffering. This is not really so very surprising because intensity of Energy often leads to obsession and single-mindedness. We are always Dynamically connected with our Enlightened Nature – so, when our Energy is highly charged with negative emotions and we have the motivation to follow ideas through to a particular end, we can create in a way that will move people. We are rarely as ecstatically happy as we are utterly miserable, so it doesn't require too much effort to understand the mechanism of *ordinary creativity* in this sense. 'Ordinary creativity' as a description of the great works of art and music could seem to be an insensitive misconception, but ordinary creativity is linked to Liberated Creativity and so genius flashes through in all manner of circumstances and in all manner of confusion. So, with ordinary creativity, there is not a lot of joyous art to be seen, heard or read. There are Vaster possible horizons of Creativity based on developing recognition of Intrinsic Space than there are in being a living disaster, even though we may leave a trail of great art in our wake.

We see the pain of desolation as our identity and maintain it by grasping for it, using the full range of our imagination to increase the pain and thereby increasing our identity. If our partner has left us for another person we anguish ourselves by imagining what they could be doing together. We imagine that they're going to all the places we used to visit together, and that they're enjoying themselves just like we used to. We deliberately imagine more and more painful scenarios as a means of bursting into tears over and over again. We might even roll around on the floor clutching at ourselves revelling in the nature of the pitiable spectacle we must appear. Our imaginary scene could continue to worsen – it could become sexually explicit to the limit of our imagination, and we'd both love and loathe what we were doing to ourselves. Having imagined things to be as bad as they possibly could be, it occurs to us that with a beautifully subtle twist the story could be worse still. So we continue until, totally exhausted by the process, we cry ourselves to sleep. There is obviously a highly perverse sense of enjoyment in all this but it's rather superficial and unreal and only serves to establish us as having the identify of 'one who is in pain'. We are saying to ourselves, "I hurt therefore I am".

Freezing as a process of dealing with pain is one in which we become hard and as cold as ice. We cut feeling out altogether and 'get on with life'. Why we just 'get on with life' we're not sure, but it's there to be lived through so that's just what we'll do. Resignation is a socially acceptable even seemingly admirable form of anger which imbues us with a false sense of dignity. It's a way of establishing our own existence through displaying that we can live without our emotions. We can't admit that we've been badly shaken with the experience of our partner leaving us: "What use are emotional relationships anyway, they've never done anyone any good." We've experienced enough of them anyway. We can even 'hold a job down', we can make the odd witty rejoinder – we refuse to let this pain touch us. We become stoic and indulge in a ludicrous kind of efficiency which is totally inept. We get on with what we are doing, knowing that no one will ever know or understand the pain we've endured and how strong we are. We bustle around our home making sure everything is immaculate, we spend our time engaged in organisational procedures which we carry out alone in order that we don't have to smile at anyone – our face locks into a frost-bitten mask of expressionlessness. Or maybe we develop an eerie fixed smile that betokens nothing and pretend that we are having a good time. We may appear to be our old selves but we're acting every minute of the time. We might even form another relationship, but if it is unable to melt the permafrost of our defences the other person becomes unable to relate to us. We're just actors or actresses and our chilly shallowness provides no communication which would enable the relationship to survive. We can't allow our new relationship to work because we cannot allow the other person near us and can't admit our pain.

Obliteration as a process of dealing with the pain of desolation is one in which we distract ourselves endlessly so that we can pretend our lover has never really left us. We attempt to take some sort of artificial holiday from our pain. Having oscillated between freezing and fantasising (which is the usual pattern), we become fatigued by the intensity of it and have to distract ourselves with all manner of entertainments. We want to engage ourselves in conversation or involvement in some kind of project or activity that will swamp our pain. We might go to night classes and learn a language or do a pottery class to re-equip our kitchen. We might do a mechanics course and try to get our car back on the road or take up painting water-colours. We call round to see friends but always with a bottle of something in tow to dull the edge of it all. We keep our diary well scheduled with events that distract us from our pain and most people imagine that we're coping quite well until we go on an almighty bender, get totally wrecked and end up keeping someone up all night weeping on them. If we can't distract ourselves we take shelter in oblivion – we get inebriated, go to sleep or commit suicide as a means of escaping what we see as the brutal reality of our situation. It's a constant process of masking off anything that hurts us.

Consolidation as a process of dealing with the pain of desolation is one in which we latch onto the fact that we have frozen our pain – we have been able to handle it! We have come through! We've endured the terrible disaster without falling apart, without even throwing a wobbly.

This encourages us to stiffen ourselves with a certain sort of morbid stolidness which grows into a sense of pride – we've certainly won our way through this time! This is our way of anaesthetising the pain. Our freezing has enabled us to avoid breaking down but now that is past we have to deal with the chilly world we have made for ourselves and in some way get to feel all right about it. We reassure ourselves that we'll certainly never let that happen again. We'll build ourselves a suit of armour which will make us invulnerable – we can get by without sensitivity. We will not allow anyone to get close to us or hurt us ever again. We become increasingly arrogant about our impregnability and vain about our having come through it all without a whimper. We despise others who break down because they don't appear to have the strength that we imagine we have.

Anticipation as a process of dealing with the pain of desolation is one of fearing the worst in advance and living in fear of what could happen. This process is always looking into the future and projecting fear further and further afield. Our partner has deserted us and we are stunned by the collapse of our territory in terms of what it means for the future. We can't rely on the future any more because our projected territory there has crumbled – we just don't know how to be in the present any more, because the future has become a howling void. We cannot make plans because our guidelines have disappeared and we feel that we've nothing to base anything on. We're not even sure who we are any more without the proximity of our partner. Our partner was part of our territory and we needed them to validate our existence.

Territory as I'm using the term here doesn't have the possessive quality of the Earth Element – territory is not regarded as a possession but as an indispensable 'sign of being'. Extension of territory doesn't have the consuming quality of the Fire Element – the annexing of experientially safe territories as secure stepping-stones in the raging river of Space is not the consummation of desire but the terrified white-knuckled grip on security. In this sense our partner had become part of us. In this frame of mind we cannot easily distinguish between 'I' and 'other' when the 'other' in question happens to be our partner. So when our partner leaves us it is as though we've undergone an amputation – our legs and arms suddenly end at the knees and elbows.

The Discovery of Space reveals another way of dealing with pain. We realise that if we don't tie our sensation of pain to our criterion of establishing our own existence (that we are permanent, solid, separate and continuous) then the pain dissolves. We have removed the conceptual scaffolding and the sensation of pain as we know it has collapsed. The process of artifically maintaining and intensifying emotional pain with thought is gyroscopic – if we keep the rings of thought constantly spinning we generate a charge that actively prevents the dissipation of our pain. Without conceptualisation, emotional pain becomes *Pure Sensation* which is Released to Dance in the Vastness of the Open Dimension of Experience. If we do nothing to or with our sensation of pain, if we just leave it as it is, it *becomes* an *Immanent-possibility* of Enlightenment. Without the strait-jacket of concept, pain ceases to be pain and becomes a Free Energy.

Needless to say, it is not easy to shed the conceptual framework and *stare into the face of arising emotions*. But we are all *Intrinsically Qualified* to do this – this Capacity is an Aspect of our Natural Condition.

In order to Liberate our perception of emotional pain of any kind we need to develop our practice of Shi-ne. We need to have Discovered our Intrinsic Space and be able to *Rest Comfortably* in that State. Without this Recognition of Intrinsic Space (which needs to be integrated with all experience) we cannot hope to completely liberate our emotions and Realise them as the Wisdom Dance of the five Khandros.

The formalised Tibetan symbol of the field of Energy is the Khorlo, the circle which transcends location, direction, form, time and space.

The colour Blue is the depth of the Sky stretching into infinity. It is Rich, Radiant and Empty, unaffected by clouds of any colour. It can also be dull, opaque, dense and flat or like smoke: impenetrable to the gaze.

This field of Energy is Unconditioned and Referenceless. There is no cardinal direction because it is all directions and no direction. Space allows the possibility of 'direction' and 'location' to manifest. It is not associated with any season or time of day because the phenomenon of time passing arises from the *Continuity of Now* – the perpetual experience of Space. Space is Vast, Infinite, Unlimited, Unoriginated and Unconditioned.

The Wisdom of Ubiquitous Intelligence and All-Encompassing Space is there as soon as we let go of the artificial process of distracted-being. It is Immediately Present when we give up struggling and indulging in the artifice of contrived relaxation. When we just 'let go' and 'let be' we Realise ourselves as Completely pen and Awake.

The practice of Shi-ne is where we start and with that we continue, using circumstances as part of our Path and Integrating Space with Sensation and Perception. Even the initial glimmerings of Intrinsic Space will enhance our ability to work with our emotions and the further we pursue the practice of Shi-ne the greater Clarity we Discover.

However, even as a psychological construct, these ideas can help us relate to the experience of emotional pain in a more *real* way. If we can connect with this View it is because already we have the experience of Intrinsic Space from Beginninglessness. It cannot help but Sparkle through the miasma of our constricted Energy.

PART THREE

Elemental Essence – Jung ('byung)

12
Discovering the Nature of the Elements

The Elements are often symbolised in the form of a Chörten, an architectural monument to the Possibility of Liberation.

The Chörten is seen everywhere in Tibet and throughout the Himalayan countries of Bhutan, Sikkim, Nepal, Lahaul, Spiti Zanskar and Ladhak. The Chörten wherever it is found, describes an exploratory movement through the Quality Spheres of the five Elements: Earth, Water, Fire, Air and Space.

The Chörten is a progression of geometric symbols which spring from each other with an elegance and simplicity that speak directly of the experiential qualities of the Elements. The Cube of Earth supports the Sphere of Water from which the elongated Cone of Fire springs upward. At the apex of the spire rides the Crescent Moon of Air in whose concave rests the Circle of Space: the Origin of the Elements.

Chörtens are made of many different materials, but the large ones that ornament the Tibetan landscape are made of stone and hardened mud. They are usually whitewashed and sometimes bear a golden Crescent of Air and Circle of Space.

I still remember the first time I saw a Chörten: the first sight of it was for me an experience completely beyond time and place; and so has remained always fresh in my mind – unclouded by the passing of time. It is as clear to me now as it was then, while the relative aspects of the journey have become lost in a fog of experiences that someone else had, a version of me that died a long time ago.

I had left the Katmandu Valley behind me by about a week and it semed as far away as my mother's garden on the other side of the world. The scenery had become alpine; I had been noticing the delicate tracery of lichen on the rocks. The brilliant sunshine effervesced at my feet in the twinkling of tiny flowers of many colours. At these altitudes you become aware that the sky above you is a window on infinity; that yawning immensity of blue opens out into Space – the Moon is often visible in broad daylight. High altitude skies are dark blue and the intensity of light that emits from them can seem quite contradictory. Colours acquire an acute poignancy in that purity of light and the blue of the sky is echoed here and there by the Tibetan blue poppies with their spiky leaves that deter the foraging mountain goats.

I was a happy wanderer in a Great Silent Place. I had one ambition: to reach somewhere to sleep the night. I was singing the seven-line Mystic Song of Padmasambhava, the Great Magician, the Second Buddha who took the Tantric Teachings to Tibet from the Mystic Land of Ögyen. Maybe he came this way, maybe he walked along this path toward Tibet subduing demons and harmonising negative influences. It would have been during the years of Charlemagne that that journey was made. Untold followers of Padmasambhava must have come this way, wandering Ngakpas singing the resonant syllables of his Awareness-spell. Maybe the sound in my ears was not just my voice alone but a harmony with the energy of the mountains which resonate with the Living Presence of Padmasambhava. I became aware that not only had my Teacher taken me into his family but that I had joined a much larger family, the White Lineage of the Lotus-Born Magician, and that all who had walked this way had been my brothers and sisters. Time seemed to melt into meaninglessness, I didn't even have a wrist-watch to remind me that I belonged to the twentieth century. The idea that I might just meet some of those amazing Tantric Heroes and Heroines I'd heard so much about seemed outrageously possible in that fantasic environment

The track, I remember, had been steep for a while. I'd sat down a few times to dangle my feet in the stream that chuckled along criss-crossing the track every once in a while. I'd eased one arm out of my maroon woollen coat – the Tibetans have various ways of wearing their chubas depending on the temperature. My bag was not too heavy, just a sun faded shoulder-bag made of the ornate cloth woven in Bhutan. Apart from my deep red blanket and shawl I only carried a few other odds and ends. I had my food and a flask of barley-beer. The food was simple – Tibetan muffins, dried apricots and the hard Tibetan cheese for chewing endlessly as you walk.

Sounds carry in the clear mountain air, the chuckling stream would guffaw as it followed the track and faded into a giggle as it took its own direction. With sun behind me I could watch the eagles circling effortlessly in the air high above.

I think it was because I'd had a short nap and a few too many rests to dangle my feet in the water that I was late reaching the next village, so I decided to put in some hard walking. I was trying to cover a few miles so I forgot about my fascination with the sky and fixed my gaze on the path. I think I must have got rather hot and was probably feeling a bit wearied so I just got my head down and harnessed my determination to reach the high point I could see – it didn't seem too far away. But the mountains can be confusing if you don't live in them and the distance to be covered taxed my physical resources more than I had expected. However, I had made some kind of commitment to myself and was obdurate about achieving my objective without resting or reducing my pace. I became oblivious to the panorama and the increasing effort focused my attention quite sharply and directly on the rhythm of my movement.

I don't really know how long it took me or even how far I walked in that determined way, but when I got to the point I'd observed from further down the track I felt rather wasted and dizzy. My heart was thumping maniacally drowning out most other sensations and dominating sensory input. I flaked out on the grass.

Some time passed before I felt able to sit up again. I can't really remember whether I went to sleep or whether I just lay there staring into the sky, but when I sat up dusk was not far off. There was a delightful refreshing fragrance that made me feel very clear and precise – the Himalayas are rich in herbs and flowers used in

Tibetan medicine.

As I sat up I saw the small whitewashed Chörten glowing against the dark but vibrant colours of the mountains. A large raven high in the air above me cawed – it was the only sound in the Universe at that moment and there was no distance between us. There was no separation between these experiences. They were a flow of free perceptions that for a while I made no attempt to direct, manipulate or interpret.

I sat wide-eyed until the familiar old patterns of perception began to re-emerge. I noticed the red sun glinting on the copper Crescent-Moon and Space-Disc of the Chörten. The Wish-Path flags flapped raggedly in the wind that had sprung up. I noticed the dusk and the lights of habitations beckoning in the near distance. They echoed the first stars speckling through the sky above the mountains, their reddening snows reflecting the sun.

I eased my free arm back into my chuba, threw my bag onto my shoulder and took the path toward the lights, glad to have spent another day in Padmasambhava's country.

I made my way down the track. I didn't turn back to have one last look at the Chörten – it didn't occur to me. I just let the bone discs of my teng'ar (rosary) slip through my fingers with my eyes fixed on the lights ahead, intoning the syllables of Padmasambhava's happy Spell: Om Ah Hung Bendza Guru Pema Siddhi Hung! joyful to have received his inspiration.

Chörten (mChod-rTen)

13
Chörten

The Chörten describes a journey through the Quality Spheres of the five Elements: Earth, Water, Fire, Air and Space.

Setting out on this journey of Discovering Openness is initiated by the exhaustion of our neurotic intentions. It is only when we can no longer fuel our neuroses that we become able to entertain some basic recognition of Space. It is only from this experience of Space that we can accept our journey or panic and retreat into a fantasised security.

Our neurotic intentions revolve around our terminal obsession to establish security at any price. We want to prove that there is something about ourselves that is solid, separate, permanent and continuous – so our neurotic intentions proliferate at every turn.

We find ourselves engaged in a bizarre balancing act. Our way of being in the world is like playing three-dimensional chess. Maybe we're also on a tightrope, or possible even on a unicycle on a tightrope. Sometimes we're winning, taking a queen with a deliciously designed move and the audience are cheering near to hysteria. Sometimes we think we've done well but the crowd are bored, they've seen it all before – so what's new about juggling with four revved-up chain-saws? So we attempt to win ourselves back into favour by making some really risky moves, but we slip and lose the game completely. We end up hanging from the tight-rope. Clinging on for grim death while watching our arch rival setting fire to the rope. Sometimes we're just too frightened to perform at all and find our security in keeping such a low profile that we stand the chance of becoming two-dimensional. We huddle in a dark corner and try to lock the world out.

These are the personal survival schemes or life-plans which we use to remove ourselves from Vast, Directionless, Timeless

Wisdom-Space: the Ground of Being.

We grab at the transient illusions of security, the glimmering reflections on the bubble of our perception that seem so solid until we try to possess them.

We attempt to fend off the transient illusions of insecurity that we imagine to be the yawning abyss of annihilation whilst we refuse to Recognise Space as the Ground of Being.

We ignore the transient illusions of apparent neutrality, the amorphous blur of a world with which we fail to connect or communicate. Where there is no immediate offer of security or imminent threat of insecurity, there is no evident possibility of direct manipulation, so we find it rather more convenient to become myopic.

Exhaustion is a state in which we are no longer able to direct our Energy, a state in which we have to relax. We all seem to experience this state every once in a while – life seems to grab us by the scruff of the neck and beat the hell out of us. We just remain suspended with our plans and schemes in ruins. It's not a great deal of fun perhaps, but when we find ourselves in this limbo we can discover that we have a lot more freedom – there is a sense of Space that we can relate to as being either threatening or inviting.

This inviting Space is our Nourishment; it allows us the possibility of regaining our impetus. We can explore the Energy of the Space we have Discovered in Relaxation, or we can recoil in fear from that Open Space. We can Open ourselves Freely to this Impetus and Discover ourselves as we Actually are, or we can impel ourselves to continue our insane struggle which we had to leave off through exhaustion.

We are free to Explore the Possibilities of Relaxation and Freedom, or retreat into the struggle to maintain the illusion of security that we have learned to engage in with its consequent constriction and suffocation.

The Chörten can be Viewed as a Journey from dense lightless claustrophobia to Intangible Self-Luminous Vastness. When we relax our efforts to substantiate ourselves we begin to recognise

Self-Existent Space – we develop the ability to explore without grasping and to question our limitations. When we struggle to substantiate ourselves we are trying to solidify Space – we are *hallucinating* non-existent confines in which we imagine we have no room to move and no time to explore. We deplete our Energies and create the *appearance of illusory confusion* in which contact with Primal Space seems to be all but lost.

Relinquishing substantiation means that we are letting go of our attempts to make Space into 'something' more acceptable to our conditioned perception. As our structured perception evaporates we realise Space as it is and ourselves as we are.

In this intellectually unimaginable *Unlearning*, the *hallucinated confines* are realised as non-existent – room to move and time to 'Be' unfold Infinitely. We realise the Inexhaustible Nature of Energy and Dance the Limitless Dance of Spontaneously-Accomplished Compassionate Activity in Primal Space.

Let's take a look at these Elements now and examine the psychological progression through them, from Earth, through Water, Fire, and Air to Space. I think it's important at this point to remind ourselves that the pattern of symbols we're going to look at in the next chapter runs parallel to the previous system rather than being an extension of it. The first symbolic pattern operated in terms of the equal yet contrasting Nature of each Element, each manifesting distracted and Liberated Energy patterns. The next symbolic pattern we are to explore traces the elements in a linear hierarchic manner, beginning with Earth as the most distracted Element and evolving through Water, Fire and Air to Space as the Liberated Element. It's therefore quite important not to attempt to interchange ideas between these systems – they function separately and don't rely on each other even though they may have certain similarities. Evans-Wentz, the famous pioneer Tibetologist, made that kind of mistake when he worked on the translation of the *Tibetan Book of the Dead* and corrected what he thought to have been mistakes in the original text where the colours and cardinal directions were at odds with the commonly used system.

There is yet another method of explaining the personality types within the Dzogchen Long-de system which uses the Elements in a different way again, but that cannot be encompassed within this particular book. The Buddhist system includes several ways of describing the variants of the human condition; in the sutras the Abhidharma talks of the five skandhas and the other sutras speak of the six realms of existence. But as with the two systems outlined in this book, they should be explored and experienced within the context of their own unique manner of functioning and not treated as the subject of comparative study.

Earth – Sa (Sa)

14
Earth

Let's look at the base of the Chörten which is a Cube – the solid Square shape of Earth.

Earth is dark, constricting and obstructive to movement. The immensity and weight of Earth doesn't allow easy movement of any kind even for the worms that gnaw their ways through the stuff. Any activity connected with the Earth Element is one of slow, blind groping. Life-forms that live in the Earth are very basic. Everything about the Earth is basic or minimal in terms of consciousness. Nothing happens at any great speed; Earth is connected with the force of gravity – a deadening inertia seems to blanket most possibilities. There is no concept of alternatives; the idea of actually Opening our Eyes doesn't seem to fall within our scheme of intense self-protectiveness – we're happy in our rhinoceros-skin overcoat.

So this is the Earth-Element state of mind and we're going to look at it through the analogy of living in a coffin and what that would or could be like. Being in the Earth-Element state of mind is finding ourselves trapped in a coffin, a cramped but padded container. We have no idea how we came to be there or why we decided that it was a good idea to immure ourselves – all we are left with is an obscure and hazy idea that at all costs we must not open the lid. At some stage beyond our recall we must have bolted solid brass handles on the inside of the lid and now, almost unaware of what we are doing, we are keeping the hatches tightly battened. So, there's no clear idea of just why we're doing this or exactly what it is that we're going to get out of it – we've lost track of the threat somewhat. It's so impenetrably dark and horribly cosy that imaginations are dormant, and the memory of whatever threat it was that made us retreat into this cossetting container is just a blur. Although our sensory input is minimal, however, we have sufficient consciousness to feel the intense stifling quality of the self-created pressure we find ourselves under. But we become increasingly unable to awaken our fear and it begins to exhaust its own neurotic intensity. There is too little possibility of comparison for our fear to be suckled and the memory of it becomes a dark mystery. When the crisp edges of our fear have become sufficiently woolly and obscure we become overwhelmed by the heaviness and claustrophobia of our environment. We lose commitment to maintaining our consciousness as a lead-lined hermetically sealed unit, we relax our grip, and surprisingly enough the lid of the coffin swings effortlessly open. There's not even a cheap horror movie ghoulish creak because the hinges are perfectly oiled just waiting to perform their natural function. We start to perceive another dimension – the possibility of physical movement. Having finally become exhausted by our own effort to exist in such a dark cramped state, we let go, we relax and an openness initiates us into some sense of Space which we could call 'the Beginning of Exploration'.

The Earth-Element personality is the sort of individual who is only capable of living in accord with set patterns. In this state of mind we know what we like because we like whatever is traditional and safe. We like it because it's traditional and it's traditional because we like it. The logic we employ is just about as subtle as that. We eat what we eat in a practical way, at the right time and in the proper place – but because we're so familiar with it we hardly taste it, let alone enjoy it. Old men tend to get a bit like this when they retire – they've lost the work routine and have become so deeply afraid of that empty space that they often lose the inclination to experiment with anything. They begin to live for mealtimes, bedtimes, and the Sunday paper. I guess you might think that reading the paper might worry our old gentleman unduly because of all the terrible chaos it conveys, but I think that would be a mistaken idea.

I remember moving into a new attic room many years ago. I was about to start a post-graduate teaching year in Cardiff and I'd decided to paint my new room white before the autumn term started. I think the landlord had tried to cheer the room up by painting it orange and yellow which made it rather like living inside an egg. My stuff was all over the floor pulled away from the walls and my radio was more or less trapped in the middle of it all and rather difficult to get at. I switched it on before I started, expecting the usual delightful classical music station I usually have it tuned to, but someone had obviously shifted the station to the one that deals mainly with news, drama and current interest features. 'Woman's Hour' was on, and there was an interview with an interesting woman who'd been to Bhutan, so I started painting and listened to that station for the rest of the day. It turned out that I listened for three days as I painted and in that time heard a lot of news. After three days I got to feel quite nervous about my future. It sounded as if life in the British Isles was going to change dramatically within weeks. The financial situation seemed so bad that I wondered what was going to happen – maybe I wouldn't even be able to start my teaching course – perhaps I'd have to return my grant and get a job dealing with ration cards. But nothing extraordinary happened at all. The world went on more or less in the same sort of way. Awful atrocities came and went but they all seemed to take place in other countries. Some years later I heard the news again and was surprised that it sounded so remarkably similar. It was equally ghastly and again I was touched very deeply by the inhumanity and the dreadful suffering in the world. But I realised that the news is there to keep people quiet – it really only serves to bombard us with catastrophe in order that a dubious status quo is maintained. The news seems to reassure us that the world around us is in ferment but that we are somehow going to be all right – the powers that be are somehow looking after us. The bombardment of the news seems to be quite a devious device because it makes us grateful for our supposed comforts whilst numbing us to problems of the wider world. The frightening television images of the world in ferment become wallpaper and leave us unaffected. The sufferings of the world become dangerously close to a total abstraction, so our old gentleman is quite secure with his newspaper – it poses no threat. It just serves to remind him that all is well, nothing is *really* changing.

This Earth-Element personality as the picture develops seems to be emerging as some sort of geriatric Victorian father. But it's not just a question of senility; there are Earth-Element people in every age group. In this state of mind we criticise any deviation from the norm because it threatens our sense of solidity and security. Our ability to question has become atrophied, our sensitivity to the world has become fossilised. The Earth-Element person is hard and scaly, inflexible, stiff in movement and humourless – you'd never see them crying with laughter or grief. But in spite of this toughness and obduracy they are very vulnerable because all the time the fluid, changing qualities of the environment are undercutting them, and the growing pain they feel has no means of expression.

I think we must all know and feel sorry for people like these. Maybe we can remember being a bit like this and maybe now we might be a bit more Water-Element based, so let's take a look at that and see what it looks like.

Although Earth is dark and confining it is the basis of growth. It is in the meeting of Earth and Water that seeds burst open and having firmly established roots, they put out shoots that break away from their dark origins.

Water – Chu (Chu)

15
Water

Above the solid Cube of Earth is the fluid Sphere of Water, the natural shape that Water assumes when it finds itself freed from the gravitational drag of the Earth. We're aware of this globular quality as part of our common experience. We've played with it as children: splashing it, watching it drip from icicles, watching it boil, blowing delicate shimmering bubbles or throwing stones out into the smooth surface of a pond to watch the attenuating circularity of the ripples. This is the nature of Water, so we're not discussing anything foreign to our experience.

Having let go of the Earth-Element state of mind we are free to discover the subtler areas that lie beyond, stretching to the perceptual horizons of our new-found capacities. This tentative field of exploration is our entry into the Water-Element state of mind. We're no longer whelking in the primeval ooze – our jellyfish mentality has been augmented by a delicate network of fins that facilitates movement.

Water allows movement, it flows itself and it flows with circumstances. The seas and the oceans of our planet respond to the power of the Moon with their tides, and to the wind with their waves and storms. Streams and rivers respond to the Earth by flowing swiftly to find the lowest level. Water responds to the phenomenal world by creating a circle and returning to its origin.

In comparison with Earth, Water makes more exact contact with the surfaces it confronts. The tides lapping the shorelines envelop every rock and every pebble – every surface is *touched* completely. When the tide ebbs it leaves an even film of moisture on every contour. The tide penetrates the sand slowly, allowing its own accommodating density to find the line of least resistance.

Water allows some vague sense of light to permeate its depths, but this is the inception of our investigation and so the possibility of looking up is not even a factor for consideration.

The movement of Water and the possible movement within Water don't present many possibilities, however, in terms of increasing the range and scope of our consciousness. It's as if we'd emerged from the dark womb of Earth and found ourselves in some dark, dank, dreary dungeon; or at the bottom of some very deep well. The Water-Element state of mind learns the gaol habit of pacing backwards and forwards easily, and so we engage in a game of 'blind man's buff' which constitutes an exploration of our environment.

We explore the surface texture of the walls with our fingers, and become absorbed with the strange character of what we are feeling. We compare textures and are even capable of guessing at the vagaries of shape in the intense gloom.

This reminds me of people studying comparative religion who never practise any method they've studied. They learn more and more about less and less and end up totally constipated with theory, understanding nothing but highly accomplished in the art of talking at great length about it. It is only possible to experience a drink by drinking it, not by comparing its colour and the shape of the glass it's been poured into with the colour of others and the shapes of the glasses into which they have been poured.

The Water-Element state of mind has few possibilities; our eyes are open, but they make little of what they see and are not attracted upward into the regions that our curious fingers are unable to grope.

At first our exploration is rather tentative, we are a trifle cautious and keep close to the ground. We make sure that at all times we keep our hands and feet firmly in contact with something solid. At some stage we stand up, alarmed and excited at the same time that we really have that much room. The excitement doesn't last long, however, because the walls at shoulder height are little different from the walls at ground level. We begin to want to make use of the Space we have found but the limits of what we feel we can do in it are narrow.

We can move from wall to wall faster and faster, but we exhaust the possibilities of exploration – there is nothing we can do in this Space but give in to the boredom of it so we lie down and relax. Now something strange happens: we have forgotten our compulsive exploration of familiar form and discovered an aspect of our environment that we hadn't even thought about before. This is something absolutely new – there is something going on above us that is not like anything we've ever seen before, some sort of lightness that intensifies as we Open ourselves to it. Suddenly we realise that there is more to our lives and our world than scrabbling about on the ground examining the nature of our faeces, peering into the fog of our confines to make sure of them as our territory. We Discover that there is more going on and more to get into than constantly identifying with our restrictions.

The Water-Element personality is found in the sort of individual who has a certain looseness about the way in which they live. They like their patterns to change from time to time. In this state of mind we know what we like and we pig-out on it until we're tired of it before going on to something else. We're interested in expanding our range of enjoyments – we want to learn the latest disco dance, we want to buy the new style of music. We want to go on a new kind of holiday, but it has to be 'the place where they're all going'. Water-Element people are dedicated followers of fashion, they've embraced change in some way, but they've done it within the bounds of fashion-culture security and dive like lemmings headlong into banality. These kinds of people look back at themselves as they were a few years ago and say: "How could I have ever gone round looking like that?" and you know that in a few years' time they'll probably be saying the same thing about how they are now.

They become followers of religion in the same way and often learn as much from it as they do from their other fashions – it's just another thing to become absorbed with. This, I am sure, is a familiar person to most of us. I am sure we could all give examples of this sort of attitude from our own experience as well as from witnessing the activities of others.

I remember someone like it myself – a visitor at a Buddhist centre where I once gave a course. He was sitting in the kitchen engaged in fraught dialogue with a young man. He was rebuking him for the flimsiness of his practice and the looseness of his morality. The young man was trying to defend himself on the grounds that Buddhism was about doing your best – but his best in the eyes of the older man was obviously not good enough. The young man was obviously rather upset, not only by the 'spiritual' assault on his 'indulgent' lifestyle but also by the level of aggression aimed at him. He used an old Zen saying to redeem himself a little in the eyes of the other. The saying went: "The person who is not on the Path has senses that are like a pack of ravening wolves. The person who is on the Path also has senses like ravening wolves but they are observed with disapproval." The older man was not at all impressed by the Zen saying, if such it was, and continued with his diatribe about karma and other pertinent topics. I found the whole thing rather sad for both of them. I was sorry for the older of the two because he was using perfectly good theory as a weapon. He had seemingly no sense of kindness, appropriateness, or any real interest in communication. His Buddhism was a bag of clichés that had come along with his new enthusiasm. I was sorry for the younger man who had only recently developed an interest in spirituality, and who felt deflated and depressed by the severity of criticism to which he'd been subjected. I talked to him afterwards and found out quite a lot about him. He was an interesting, enthusiastic person who had only just started to question the meaning of his life, and what he really needed was encouragement. He'd obviously gone out on a limb coming to this place as it was, and in doing so he'd put himself in a no man's land between acceptance by new friends and the falling away of old ones. He was in a delicate situation and needed someone friendly to talk to.

I met the other man a few years later in a Mind, Body, Spirit Festival. He had left his wife and children for a member of a rather sinister cult. Now he was handing out leaflets advocating free love as a way of bringing people to God – he'd obviously forgotten all about karma.

There could be many such stories and I'm sure that some of you must be thinking of them at this moment.

Although water is viscose and clinging, it is the basis of ascendancy. It is through the meeting of Water with Fire that the shoots of plants grow upward into a new dimension and burst into flower in dazzling array.

Fire – Me (Me)

16
Fire

Above the Sphere of Water is the Cone of Fire. Fire is Conical or Triangular in shape because it surges upward from a base, gradually becoming more attenuated until only delicate flickering tongues are left at the apex.

Fire is dynamic and in a certain sense reckless and unruly, although it conforms to its own inhibitions. Fire is an enthusiastic Energy that moves in an upward direction at the expense of its surroundings. It has an insatiable, manic quality – it seems driven by a wild passion that wants to make love to the sky. It indiscriminately burns the objects of its fascination and constantly needs more fuel. Fire is bright, gaudy and alive but it is also obsessive and destructive. The innate enthusiasm of Fire is always over-reaching itself – often dramatic forks of flame leap so far from the conflagration that they become separated and dissipate having lost their connection. In order to ascend, Fire has to exhaust the elements below it. So Fire is limited – its apex depends completely on its base. When its fuel runs out the Fire dies. Because Fire is so obsessed with climbing it neglects its fuel supplies and exhausts itself – it could never burn the whole world to a cinder because its perspective is too narrow. It's a short-lived phenomenon that remains constantly unsatisfied.

The Fire-Element state of mind displays the first sparks of excitement. We have just discovered that there is no roof to our prison. This is a new and intriguing idea which enthralls us with the spirit of adventure – we want to be consumed in a welter of discovery and so we leap into the Fire of this new upward direction. We begin to jump – we can see the sky! We can also see those tantalising wispy cirrus clouds constantly metamorphosing in it. Sometimes we can see immense voluptuously billowing cumulus clouds moving in and out of our frame of vision. Sometimes birds fly across – twittering sparrows or great white eagles gliding effortlessly in an Element that is infinitely mysterious to us. We want to get closer – we try to scale the wall of our prison but the footholds are too narrow and we slip. There are better ledges higher up but there seems to be no way at all of reaching them even if we jump with all our effort. It's all beyond our reach and it's diabolically frustrating to say the least.

We try different approaches of making sense of this new dimension by trying to record our impressions of it. Sometimes it's light, sometimes it's dark and there's a time in between when one is exquisitely gradating into the other. When it's dark there are twinkling pin-points of light, stars whose patterns change very slowly as the night rolls by, and even more slowly still as the seasons follow each other. The Sun and Moon come into vision as well and for every new thing we see, our picture gets more complicated – it's completely bewildering! If only we could climb up there into it – maybe we'd see the whole picture and understand what it meant. Maybe we'd then be *whole beings* who'd got the measure of it all – it would be ours and we could govern its functioning.

Inevitably everything that we see only serves to tantalise us. Every time we feel we may have some understanding a greater sense of mystery is aroused. We always seem to be at the threshold of some Greater Knowlege but are inexplicably jilted. It's as if we are on tip-toe reaching for some priceless object but every time we are about to grasp it, the rug is pulled from beneath our feet and we crumple into an ignominious heap on the floor. Our excitement is quite out of touch with what's really going on and can't connect genuinely with what is actually unfolding all around us. This excitement of ours has too much of the quality of hunger and desperation about it. Our desire to see more has grown into a driving fixation and we injure ourselves in our reckless attempts to get 'closer' to this 'mystery'.

Finally, exhausted by the struggle, we can no longer sustain the intensity of our quest. In this exhausted state we may well just sit on the ground and relax, but in that moment something strange might happen. In that moment of giving up there could be a glimpse – a moment of Openness and the recognition of Intrinsic-Space. Contacting this Space gives us room for the idea to occur that there may be other avenues of exploration. We may perceive that the walls of our prison are not quite as substantial as we had imagined. They were the confines of our world after all and could easily have been several thousand miles thick or even have stretched into infinity. Throughout our tentative attempts at furtive feeling through to our reckless and abandoned jumping and climbing we have in fact dislodged a few stones here and there. There seem to be chinks of light between some of the stones. Suddenly our Energy returns and we can begin to work with these loosened stones. We don't have to work too hard or too fast, because we've developed a degree of respect for this new possibility – in fact we are ever so slightly awe-struck about what we might find. Our exploration is no longer based on preconceptions about what it is that we're going to find.

We are looking at our world and at ourselves in a way so different that it invites us to take a quite different line of approach to our environment and the nature of our relationship to it. We discover the possibility of being patient and thorough – we are working with care because we have no real concept of what could happen. This brings to mind the image of an archaeologist working with a sable brush in order not to damage the rare thing that might lie beneath the sand in some pyramid. We find that these prison walls are not actually that strong in places and so we work in a determined way – approaching our endeavour more Openly and Accurately. We begin to learn things about the nature of the walls and the best way to loosen the stones. We become familiar with the different aspects of the stones in terms of how their function relates to us. We discover in addition that these stones have functions which are not entirely dependent on our fevered desire to manipulate. Soon we have a window which we widen until we are faced with the choice of whether we really want to climb out of it or not.

The Fire-Element personality is the sort of individual who has a great deal of nervous Energy. They can often be highly risky people to be around. They love to take chances, to live fast and furiously and involve people in the risks they take. They like their patterns like the Earth- and Water-Element people, but they like to have them in order to deviate from them. In this state of mind we want all kinds of different food in all sorts of imaginative combinations, we want the best quality food. "We don't know what we want but we want it now!" We are impulsive in our actions - everything has to happen immediately. Whatever we do, we do with great gusto, panache and verve but halfway through we've got something else in mind that could be better. We are continually gearing ourselves up for the next thing; we constantly want to be 'where it's at', where it's really happening. We've run the best race, completed the fastest ski run in the world, but while the applause is still in ferment we're thinking about next year – always on to the next thing.

A lot of people would seem to admire us for what we appear to be achieving or accomplishing but it's all rather hollow because we never actually get anywhere or do anything at all. It's an external theatre of missing the target – never really *Being* in what we are doing. Externally it's a remarkable show, a fantastic hit record, but internally there's some sort of hollow chasm that's echoing with whispers of frustration and failure. Nothing ever works out to be quite as good as we feel it could or should be. An awful niggling doubt pursues us that this might be all there is to life! So we continue to ride the same neurotic pattern of Energy with the hope that one day we'll hit the high from which we'll never come down. We're very electric and personal contact with us can be fatal – close friends and lovers seem to sustain emotional third-degree burns when their lives cross ours. In the end we short-circuit ourselves, but in the meantime the next mountain we climb will be higher – we'll choose a more difficult slope. The next car will be faster, the next lover might just make the Earth move, the waves might really come crashing in like they do in the films. We are going all out for peak experiences – we'll do it if it kills us.

There are many different angles to this story-line; instead of being an athlete, mountaineer, brain surgeon, scientist, or stunt-person, we might find ourselves on the less acceptable side of the fence. We could be a hell-raiser, a gambler or some sort of daredevil drug-fiend hooked on riding the great brain liquidiser in search of the ultimate hallucination that will answer *all* the questions. We could go further out still and be gangster, hit-man, gun-runner or mercenary. Even further out and we could be a psychopath, a mass murderer without limit.

In religious terms we could be fanatics – we could have been at the forefront of the Spanish Inquisition. We could have been part of the witch hunts with a fevered desire to burn anybody for almost any reason. We could be spiritual extremists specialising in mortification of the flesh. Or in a milder vein we could be evangelists roaring fire and brimstone at tremulous congregations or wanting to convert the world to whatever it is that we happen to believe in. We get our 'high' out of whipping people into a frenzy and feeding on that Energy. I suppose there is no limit to the examples. A lot of people we might admire have something of this quality about them – we are all attracted to peak experience. Some of us go for it ourselves while others prefer to read about it or watch it from a safe distance – living on the vicarious 'highs' of literary and cinema thrills and spills. Maybe we'd all really like to be a hero or heroine. Maybe some of us are from time to time – it's an Energy that we all have. But maybe there's another way to be – a way that finds the peak without actually trying to reach it. I'm talking about a way that isn't looking for the peak to be anywhere or any time other than where we are at every moment, Here and Now. When we exhaust the neurosis of seeking and it occurs to us to find our 'peak' within our Being we enter the Air-Element.

Although Fire is a rampant, ravenous Energy it is the basis of our inquisitiveness. It is in the meeting of Fire and Air that plants produce fruit of many vivid colours that ripen in the Sun.

Air – Lung (rLung)

17
Air

Above the Cone of Fire is the Crescent Moon of Air. Air is a Crescent Moon rather than a Full Moon because it is not the entire story, even though it seems to resemble it. Air shows us a lot about freedom, but the Whole, Vast, Limitless meaning of Complete-Freedom is eclipsed – not Entirely Illuminated.

Air moves over the surface of our deliriously beautiful, magical planet in every direction. It explores the other elements without fear of contamination. It explores with far greater freedom than Earth could ever imagine. Earth is static and rigid, having no concept at all of anything outside its own confines. The Air-Element could be said to be beyond the wildest dreams of Earth, but Earth doesn't have particularly wild dreams at the best of times.

Air explores with greater freedom than Water because although Water makes more exact contact than Earth, it envelops its objects of exploration whilst to a certain extent being oblivious of them. It smothers them – blankets them out.

Air explores with greater freedom than Fire because although Fire has an extraordinarily intimate relationship with all its objects of exploration, it consumes them in order to fuel further exploration and never really honestly knows them. Fire is more concerned with coercion then appreciation – more intent on rape than making love.

Air glances over surfaces often leaving no trace at all of its having done so. Although Air can be a destructive gale, hurricane or tornado we are not considering it here in such dramatic terms. To most of us these violent aspects of the Air-Element are infrequent – we are used to milder conditions. We are used to fairly strong winds, the kind that invigorate us – people sometimes talk about such a wind 'blowing the cobwebs away'. We are even more familiar with light winds and gentle breezes wafting through the trees. In the whispering Dance that such a wind has with trees, very little is changed – if a leaf falls it is because it is in its nature to do so. We cannot blame the wind for that, can we? Watching the lively but gentle fall of leaves in the Autumn we know that the time is ripe for this to happen – the wind is certainly not the sole cause of what is happening.

Air needs no solid base like Fire and so is not restricted to its point of origin. Strictly speaking, Air has no point of origin – only a destination. Low-pressure areas suck wind toward them from high-pressure areas – but I don't want to get too meteorological about this. Air is largely unimpeded by the world. It cannot pervade everything but that is of little consequence to the wind – its direction is not obstructed. Air is light and invisible unless it carries dust or smoke along with it, but inevitably whatever attempts to adhere eventually falls away. Air is subtle and present everywhere – our world has a complete atmosphere of it that moves in fantastic patterns according to the many fluctuations that prevail.

The Air-Element state of mind has a great deal of liberty – its explorations are sensitive and gracious but nevertheless, very Direct and Impeccably Precise. So we have climbed out of our prison with a certain degree of care and apprehension – we have removed the stones and have climbed out through the window that we have made. We probably spent some time gazing in amazement through the window before we took the plunge – but now we're here outside and it's almost unbelievably delightful. We have walked out into a world that has always been there and we can't help smiling at it and at ourselves. The smile gets broader and broader – we turn around to take a look at the vast and mighty dungeon in which we were imprisoned and realise that it's only a very small and insignificant part of the landscape. It's already derelict and as time rolls on we see that it will collapse and fall apart completely – it's a biodegradable structure that will dissolve into the landscape. When we discover that we create our own sense of unfulfilment and sustain it only through constant effort, we may well burst out laughing! This is all really very funny because we realise that we built this little hidey-hole in the first place. Our Laughter is such Good Healthy Laughter that the reverberations cause what remains of the bizarre little edifice to collapse into a pile of rubble.

We are now free to take a stroll anywhere we choose. It's all so inviting, so magnanimously accommodating and hospitable. The landscape is abundant – overflowing with fascination. But unlike the fascination of the Fire-Element we can touch without possessing - we can touch, experiencing the infinitely varied textures. We can taste the berries that glisten and glow in the bushes, in fact they seem to beckon us. We can smell the delicious scent of the pine forests; hear the melodious Songs of the Water and of the wind in the tree branches above our heads. We can see it all – we can see so many different intriguing spectacles disporting themselves all around us and it's completely exhilarating! We've certainly never seen anything like this before – not even in the most lurid dreams of our Fire-Element state of mind. We almost don't know where to look first, but we know that there's all the time in the world at our disposal and that the world has all our time as well. It's a relationship – a Dance in which we feel a sense of Equality and Friendship with everything.

It's a very free situation because we have so few demands and because we're not out to dominate anything. We are enraptured – spellbound by the fabulous green rolling hills that climb into the horizon, row upon row in graduated shades of green. Beyond and all around are majestic blue mountains that seem to pierce the blueness of the sky itself. The sight of them is breath-taking, and they're ornamented with pristine snows that reflect the changing colours of the sky.

Sometimes they are wreathed in clouds, sometimes shrouded in mysterious swirling fogs. The Sun rises and sets, changing from rich expansive yellow to white-gold, and mellowing through orange into the seductive vibrancy of red. Everything speaks to us personally – we are able to experience poignantly the Blueness of Blue, the Whiteness of White, the Yellowness of Yellow, the Redness of Red and the Greenness of Green. The shades and tonal varieties seem to have no end because every colour seems to have the other four colours within it just as every Element is interpenetrated by every other Element. We can appreciate all this because we are not that possessive, we can let every situation arise freshly and dissolve with little regret.

There are waterfalls and cataracts. There are rivers, streams and brooks whose endless tinkling sounds fill the air with their music. There are ponds and lakes in whose sparkling waters the fins and scales of golden fish glint in the sunlight. Sometimes the water dances with the wind, and sometimes it's smooth and clear, reflecting the vastness of the sky.

Animals graze, frolic in the grass or lie in the shade of trees. They run, jump or scurry away from sight – but others appear in splendid profusion. There is bird-song in the air that trills down from the high leafy branches of trees – the comical conversation of frogs among the reeds at the lake's edge, and the almost imperceptible gossamer flittering of butterflies. Every sense perception is enchanted.

The Air-Element state of mind is one in which we are free and almost unrestricted – but our last limitation is very subtle indeed. The possibility of Expanding our openness and freedom Beyond this is inconceivable to us – totally incomprehensible. No earthly frame of reference could allow us to imagine such an utterly boggling possibility, apart that is, from our Experience of Intrinsic-Space. So, we need to Free ourselves from our sense of freedom. This may be difficult to understand, but it is actually this astonishing environmental freedom which is constraining us. Our attachment to fascination encourages us to indulge in our perception without Opening ourselves to the Unconditioned Space in which perception Arises. Inevitably our fascination covers up a subtle sense of anxiety – traces of boredeom – traces of doubt – traces of even the slightest fear. If we Recognise this subtle bewilderment – if we allow ourselves to confront our bewilderment at the Sheer Variety of perceptual phenomena we may exhaust our need to maintain ourselves as observers of infinite perceptual input. As we relax in this condition it could occur to us that the last vestige of our prison is still beneath our feet.

When we left our prison we thought we'd said goodbye to captivity and bondage, but now it becomes evident that whether we are on one side of the wall or the other makes little difference in ultimate terms. The entire world has become our prison. We may have laughed before, but this really is the most outrageous joke there ever was – the final Cosmic Joke. It dawns on us that we can make anything into a prison depending on whether we manipulate it as a reference point or not. We realise that we can Allow any situation to Free itself, simply by Letting go of our reference points.

At this stage, if we are able to *embrace* insecurity, the ground loses its hold and the Dynamic Vastness of Space becomes Open to us. We are now able to move in any direction without obstruction. Our Fascination is a free Non-clinging Fascination – an Absolute Appreciation that Resonates Sympathetically with Everything. Perception and Objects of Perception melt into the Unified Field of our Being and we Instantaneously Realise that it has always been like that. The boundaries Dissolve and the subject–object dichotomy Evaporates into the Natural Play of Unconditioned Potentiality.

Air-Element personalities are very Powerful and very Interesting. They exist in all cultures or at least have existed in all cultures. Wherever they are to be found they are recognised as Special People. Some are very Special People indeed and are known as Mystics, Lamas, Medicine-people, Shamans, Sufis, Wizards, Witches, Witch-doctors, Sorcerers, Magicians, Yogins, Yoginis, Seers, and Saints . There are many more names for these people than these because they have existed in all societies and at all times throughout history.

It's not easy to say much about these people because psychologically they are outside most people's frame of reference altogether. It's really only possible to discuss how they appear – but that is not such a simple matter either, because they seem different in the eyes of different people. Some of them have either discovered Space and are Integrating it with as many moments of their lives as they can Open themselves to. Some of them have just Discovered Space or are in the process of Discovering it.

Those who are just starting out on the Journey into the Experience of Space are certainly Great People to be around – they have a certain Confidence and a Relaxed style of Being. They can be kind, generous and seem to be able to ride the vicissitudes of life with far greater ease than other people. Those who have Journeyed further are something else completely. From my own experience they can be very gentle and warm whilst some can seem quite stern. Some can appear to be flamboyant or outrageous, but usually in a way that teaches you something important. There is no stereotype – they're all different. But on the other hand, there's something about them that's identical but which you could never call typical because it can never genuinely be imitated – it's too indefinable. I think I'll tell a story at this point, and I hope that it will illuminate what I'm getting at.

I remember once in Tso-Pema, a small settlement in the Himalayas of north India, that a very strange and inspiring event took place.

Tso-Pema which means 'Lotus-Lake' in Tibetan, is a very special place to the Nyingma Tradition of Tibet. It is the place where the Tantric Buddha Padmasambhava was to be burned alive on a pyre by the King of Zahor, because the King's daughter, Princess Mandarava, had become Padmasambhava's pupil and Mystic Consort. The texts relate that Padmasambhava worked some magic with the Elements and the pyre became the lake of Tso-Pema. As you can imagine, the King of Zahor was suitably impressed. Amazed by the miracle he gave up his ignominious designs on the life of the Second Buddha and became his pupil instead. So this Wondrous Lake is there today, not particular spectacular to look at, perhaps, especially at first sight, but it is the home of a miraculous occurrence which is easier probably for us to relate to than Padmasambhava's wonder-working because it happens now.

Every year on Padmasambhava's Birthday, and also at other Special times important to him, a small floating island (the remnant of the pyre) circumambulates the lake, and that is something truly incredible to witness. It's not some great secret for the eyes of the highly realised alone or for the very special – anyone can go there at that time and see it. Maybe deciding to go there makes you a bit special anyway – I don't know.

Once His Holiness Dudjom Rinpoche the head of the Nyingma Tradition was there for this wonderful occasion and many Ngakpas came from all over the Himalayas to be there with him. They all congregated to perform rites in the Nyingma Monastery of Lama Könchog Rinpoche, with His Holiness Dudjom Rinpoche presiding. The monks were on one side of the temple and the Ngakpas on the other. The monks all looked alike, being dressed in the same traditional maroon and yellow robes comprising voluminous skirt, waistcoat and shawl that leaves the right arm exposed. But their faces, their expressions were all different – their experiences of life told differently on their faces and in their eyes. They were kind, sad, humorous, happy, peaceful faces that made my heart glad to see them. On the other side were the Ngakpas, all dressed differently – an altogether outrageous gathering of people. Some with hair wound round tubular silver containers on the crowns of their heads – these are called 'Takdrol' which means 'liberation on wearing', and are filled with Awareness-spells and power-substances. Some with alarming quantities of hair coiled up on their heads – some Ngakpas have been known to have hair that stretched to over fifteen feet in length. There were some with buns, pig-tails, plaits or just freehanging matted tousels. Some wore the white, red and blue striped shawls of the Ngakpa Tradition whereas some had maroon and some white shawls. Some wore the voluminous white cotton skirts called shamthabs pleated front and back, whilst some wore maroon shamthabs and still others wore sunfaded maroon or black serge chubas from Tibet. Some had wispy moustaches, some chin-whiskers and one or two full beards which are very rare among Tibetans. Some wore conch-shell spiral earrings and meditation-straps across their chests, slung from the right shoulder and wound under the left arm. They all looked quite different, but one thing was startlingly similar – their Eyes! They all had large wide Open Clear Eyes, and they were all the same. It was almost as if I was under the scrutiny of birds of prey, but the Eyes were not predatory they were just taking Everything in without judgement. I sat down with them with some feeling of trepidation which was soon cut through when the old Ngakpa next to me give me a mischievous grin and tugged on my beard.

I suppose that is what I mean when I say that the outward manifestation may be different but the Inner Experience is the same. I think maybe we have noticed something of this quality in the sincere practitioners of many traditions – especially among those who have given up philosophy in favour of Direct Experience. I think that we all would like to partake of that Experience and cultivate it for the well-being and benefit of everyone.

Although Air has the vestiges of limitation, it is the threshold of Space. Our atmosphere thins out at its upper reaches and finally merges into what we know as outer space. However, the Space I refer to (as it applies within our Being) could be called Inner Space – the beginning and end of everything.

It is in the meeting of Air and Space that the Fruits are harvested, shared with others and eaten with Great Enjoyment.

Sky/Space – Kha (mKha')

18
Space

Above the Crescent-Moon of Air is the Empty-Disc of Space.

Space is a Circle with no centre and no periphery.

Space is the Beginningless, Endless Source of Everything.

Chörten

19
Metamorphosis of Shape

If we look at the shapes of the Elements in the Chörten in terms of how they evolve into each other we find another analogy for discovering Primal Space.

A Cube has a *massiveness* about it that makes it almost ungainly in appearance – its boundaries seem very sharply defined. It's a very unyielding shape – there's not a lot of softness or compromise about it. The natural evolution of the Cube is toward Expansion, and when it becomes willing to compromise, its edges blur – the sharp straight lines bend and the angular corners melt into a homogeneous surface. The Cube softens into a Sphere.

But a Sphere is somewhat isolated and directionless until it moves beyond its circumference. Every direction we move on a Sphere is the same direction and leads back again to the same point. Its Natural evolution is to take a direction from itself or of itself – the Sphere becomes a Cone.

The Conical focusing shape that Energy assumes is continually re-focusing itself – continually on the move. The intensity of the Conical energy is always focusing on something but the focus is always shifting from one thing to another – it never actually burns through its object of focus. Its Natural evolution is toward relaxed attention, so when the desperation and the intensity flags, the object of attention *Vanishes* in the single pointedness of concentration – the rays of light diverge. If we imagine this Cone to be like a light beam we could make a photographic analogy. We could say that if the lenses in our camera weren't aligned to create an image – if there was no divergence produced by the lenses from the convergence of light rays, our slide show would just be an interminable series of white dots on the screen. That might seem pretty avant-garde to some, but the interest would soon pall. So, when the Cone allows itself to diverge again a very interesting picture forms – the Crescent-Moon. The Crescent-Moon is still within the realm of duality which is evidenced by its two horns. The Crescent-Moon has a noticeable perimeter, a convex edge that tapers into nothing, and a concave edge that is invitingly Open. It is that very Openness that allows the possibility of finally letting go of all constraints. When this occurs the Crescent is entirely Opened out into a Centreless Radiant fringe of Light that pervades Inner and Outer Space.

We could say that the Cube was the body, the Sphere the eye, the Cone the field of sight, the Crescent-Moon the lens, and the Empty-Disc the Vision.

Uncovering the Essential Nature – Ngo-dre-wa (Ngo-sbrad-ba)

20
Multiplicity of Analogies

Although the Movement through the Elements of the Chörten has been described as an ascending scale it can obviously also be a descending scale.

Exhaustion leads to giving up. Giving up leads to relaxation in which the Recognition of the Experience of Intrinsic Space can occur. Whenever we find ourselves confronted by Space we have two alternatives – we can either Embrace insecurity or we can retreat from it. This happens all the time in our lives – the pull and push between the known and the unknown.

Insecurity both *invites* and threatens us; likewise, security both lures and stifles us. We can always either take a chance or settle for an easy option.

If we have no guidance and if we are completely isolated we would have little chance of journeying upward through the Quality Spheres of the Elements. We need to be reminded, and we need to remind ourselves of how important it is to find our security in insecurity. We need to remind ourselves of this every day, every time we are about to grab at illusory security at the expense of an uncertain but exciting new departure from the norm. We need to digest the notion of Intrinsic Space and to Actualise it through the practice of Shi-ne. Only if we cultivate a *familiarity* with Intrinsic Space can we flow with it to any extent in our daily lives. When clinging to habitual patterns exhausts us we need the Recognition of Intrinsic Space to enable us to take the risk of shedding the security of our habits.

The life of the practitioner is a series of barriers behind which we would like to be secure, and our practice is to allow them to dismantle themselves in the Experience of Space like a snake uncoiling its own knots.

From the condition of Air we may retreat in sheer panic from the Vastness of Space. We may be so disturbed by it that we start to rebuild our prison from the rubble we left behind. At first we use it as a shelter from inclement weather but our real motive is to shield ourselves from the Experience of Openness. Rationalisation becomes rampant – we devise a multitude of very reasonable excuses that are actually very dangerous to our growth: "After all it would be safer in there and we could always leave a window to climb out of again once we'd fortified ourselves." But we're fortifying our fear habit rather than our Openness. So our fear gnaws away at us and we make our window smaller and smaller until it's entirely bricked up and all we are left with is our little chimney-hole of vision.

From the condition of Fire that we have re-created from the plethora of experience which is the Air-Element, we grasp at security even more avidly. We are rather too nervous of those Experiences of Space that seem to lie in wait in every situation. We would seem to have reconstituted the habit of missing the point as a way of life and fail to Realise that it is exactly because Space is in every situation that there is no hiding from it forever. We smoulder in our nervousness and attempt to block our thoughts of the other end of the chimney. But Space is behind everything everywhere – it's even part of our dull ashes. So we fill the chimney with smoke to obscure the sky and find ourselves in the condition of the Water-Element.

We have retreated from the possibilities of the dimension of Fire – we don't even want to draw attention to ourselves with those give-away smoke signals. Someone might home in on us and drag us out into the Open again. We want to remain perfectly still and inert. We want to cut out all insinuations of insecurity and in doing so we create the monolithic crypt of the Earth-Element. We want to barricade all in-roads and remove all risk of exposure to dimensions of Being in which we feel we could not exist.

So this is the Earth-Element again, we have returned to our nuclear bunker and the last sound we hear for quite some time is going to be the heavy dull thud of the lead shields cutting us off from all input of any kind. As far as our consciousness is concerned this is where we are, but the other people who skip past us wonder who we are and why we're sitting there hunched up when we could be enjoying ourselves.

Each point of relaxation is a somewhat outrageous challenge that we can either meet with courage or reject through fear that we may cease to exist. So, it's important to develop and Realise the View that we are continuously ceasing to exist and continuously re-emerging from Emptiness.

We have looked at all kinds of analogies which attempt to point a finger at the Moon of Liberation. It is important however that whether the finger is gloved, whether it is a Tibetan finger, a Cherokee finger or a Caucasian finger; that what is Important is not the finger but the Moon.

There are a myriad apt and pertinent analogies that Spring Effortlessly to Mind when considering the Elements – they are as Inexhaustible as Experience. So whether we discuss different kinds of prison, landscape, weather conditions or methods of transport makes little difference. Everyone will have their own preferences that Arise from their Unique Eexperience and the Nature of their Individual Energies.

The personal pictures I have painted of the Elements probably seem to leave a lot of personalities out. I'm sure that this must be apparent to anyone. I'm sure we all know people who cross the boundaries of several Elements in terms of the descriptions we've discussed. The pictures are basic because just as Space permeates every Element so do the other Elements permeate each other. Each Element contains the other Elements within it.

There are Water, Fire, Air and Space qualities of Earth. There are Earth, Fire, Air and Space qualities of Water, and so on. Nor do we always exist continuously in one specific mode – we fluctuate constantly. We change according to the Nature of the Dance between the patterns of our perception and the phantasmagorical theatre of the phenomenal world.

This is a very subtle psychology and it is not intended that we squeeze people into categories of any kind. People categorise themselves in excruciatingly varied ways without our assistance, so it is expressly not the legitimate activity of any spiritual practitioner to get off on indexing them as a pseudo-spiritual pastime. It is up to us to Observe ourselves and work with how we happen to find ourselves. It is up to us to discover our own Clarity so that we can expose our own categories of indirect-experience – our fear of Space and our sneaky yearning for security.

This book could be significantly longer – maybe we could have looked at all the possible personality subdivisions: the Fire/Air person, the Water/Earth person and so on. But really that would have been vaguely insulting. We all have the Intrinsic Capacity of Clarity that can be Awakened with the practice of Shi-ne.

We can discover these things for ourselves and discover our own analogies based on our own Rich histories of Experience.

Ecstasy – Dewa (bDe-ba)

21
Dance of the Five Wisdom Sisters

The Earth-Element's distorted perception reflects *solidity*; Its projections manifest as intractable static obduracy.

The Water-Element's distorted perception reflects *liquidity*; Its projections manifest as viscosity – adhering to familiar form.

The Fire-Element's distorted perception reflects *ascendency*; Its projections manifest as hunger for discovery – omniverous craving for knowledge.

The Air-Element's distorted perception reflects *motility*; Its projections manifest as freedom from inhibition – seduced by variety – intoxicated by fascination for the shine on the passing moment.

The Undistorted Space-Vision Reflects Emptiness; Vibrant, Self-Luminous Vastness. Free from Enlightenment and non-Enlightenment. Source of Limitless obstructed and Unobstructed Phenomena. Space Manifests Spontaneously Self-Arisen, Self-Accomplishing Compassionate Activity. This Ground of Being is the Groundless-Ground from which the appearances of the phenomenal world arise and dissolve – Self-Liberated from Beginninglessness.

Shining Emptiness! Great Mother! Heart Essence of the Elements, Dance of the Five Wisdom-Sisters.

PART FOUR

Dorje-tröllo

22
Method

So, now we have a picture – a picture made up of pictures: a kaleidoscopic image. But unless we can make use of it, it becomes a phantasmagoric mental game. Unless this picture is to remain a gossamer of meta-psychological poetry we must have a way of integrating this Vision of Being into our everyday lives. This after all is what this book sets out to encourage.

The final chapter then is about what we can actually *do* ourselves. It's about making use of the material in this book in order that we can work with our emotions. To simplify this as much as possible I have included a diagram which show the essentials of the five styles of emotional habit pattern, and recapitulate the essential stages of Method. You'll find this diagram at the end of this chapter.

So, let's take a look at where we can start.

Firstly, the View is very important – we need to assimilate what we've read. The only way I know of achieving this is through repeated rereading. If the material *makes sense*, if it *resonates* with us then remembering won't be a problem. In order to *Know* this material we have to *See* it reflected in ourselves – it has to stop being external information and start to become Knowledge that we Discover in ourselves. Some sort of synapse has to spark between the *Point-Instant* of our Perception and the manifested emotion with which we have become involved.

So, firstly we need to familiarise ourselves with the pattern and meaning of the ideas presented.

Secondly we need to *See* what we recognise of the ideas in ourselves. We should perhaps ask ourselves these questions: "Does this pattern of emotional styles correspond with my experience?"; "Can I understand my own emotions presented in this particular way?"; "Am I prepared to Discover that my emotions function in this way?" If our answer are all "Yes", then we can proceed. If our answers are all "No", then we can still proceed, but in some other way – there are many Paths to follow in the world. Answering "No" means that no correspondence has been found with the material as I've presented it. This is no reflection on the Essential Nature of the material but rather on my personal vision and my style of explanation. There are many different styles of presenting the patterns of our energies and not everyone will find themselves 'in tune' with the presentation they've found here as I've expressed it. Even within one specific system, the styles of explanation vary according to personality and the nature of individual experience.

Working with View means that we are Opening ourselves to See the five-fold expressions of distracted-being as being the warp and weft of our life's experience. Working with View means that we have the *Capacity* to See our everyday lives as a web of opportunity in/through which we can Realise the five-fold expressions of Liberated-Being.

Firstly we are familiarising ourselves with the View.

Secondly we are Internalisng the View through Experience.

The third step is to accept the challenge of *deliberately naming* our feelings of negativity, frustration, dissatisfaction, and emotional pain as *doorways* to new Experiences of Being.

As soon as we recognise a negative emotion arising we need to *look* at it and examine its 'qualities'. Let's take an example: if it is anger we are feeling then we know that this emotional energy is based on a fear reaction to Space. Our reaction to Space has been such that we have *en-visioned* it as a hostile force. In terms of re-cognisable everyday consciousness we become angry when we fear our world – we are insecure and need to take violent action to 'save' ourselves. We seem to 'know' that our best form of defence is attack and that our instantaneous reprisals or calculations for reprisals are quite justifiable. Our perception of the 'strike-potential' of others is magnified by our feelings of fear, our inadequacy and insecurity. We have to lash out – make examples to let people know that we have teeth. We hope that people will imagine that our bite is worse than our bark. Violence ranging from door slamming and verbal vitriol to physical assault become the arsenal of our response to the world.

Every time we see ourselves conforming to part of the five-fold pattern of distracted-being we distance ourselves from the artificial intensity of what we are feeling. When we are able to see ourselves operating in impersonal pre-ordained ways we can no longer take it all so seriously. Recognising any negative emotion as a perceptual habit gives us a little breathing space. It's almost as if we've been in some stuffy overheated room but it has occurred to us to open the windows wide – there is straight away a feeling of Spaciousness that we would do well to cherish and respect as an expression of our *Innate Dignity* as human Beings. This is our first Experience of Space Sparkling through the knotted web of our conditioning. Learning to be suspicious of our negative emotions and the seriousness which we invest in them is a very powerful attitude to adopt, and one that can enable us to learn from everyday experiences.

As soon as we Realise that what we are experiencing as a negative emotion is not really particularly individual or personal we may be able to let go of a degree of attachment to it. Surrendering even a fractional degree of attachment is acknowledging that we are prepared to work with our emotions.

Once we have recognised the habitual patterning of any emotion we need to Open ourselves to the *Intrinsically Inviting Opportunity* to *Stare* at it.

Firstly we Familiarise ourselves with the View.

Secondly we Internalise the View through Experience.

Thirdly we Prepare ourselves with the intention of catching ourselves out in the act of conforming to pre-set emotional patterns.

Fourthly we Stare into the face of the arising emotion.

In order to Stare at the arising emotion we have to give up our intellectual analysis immediately we recognise the emotional patterning. It is enough that we have Recognised the pattern – we don't have to dwell in intellectual analysis once that faculty has performed its useful task. I mean to say; we can dig up potatoes with a spade but once they're on our plate the spade becomes pretty redundant and if we insist on using it to eat our food we will encounter difficulties of a ludicrous order. The intellect is a valuable tool but unless we learn when to use it and when not to use it, the View with which we have familiarised ourselves will just become another unhelpful adjunct to the giddying whirlpool of our conditioned responses.

To give up analysis means to Stare Directly into the face of the emotion. We can accomplish this by making the sensation of the emotion the subject/object of our meditation. We should focus our whole attention on the wordless sensation of our emotion. If the emotion we are working with is one of sorrow, we tend to feel this as a very real and uncomfortable sensation just beneath the rib-cage. This is what is commonly known as 'heartache'. If we are able to let go of the words, the conceptual scaffolding, then the sensation ceases to manifest as pain and, if we can maintain the presence of our attention, becomes a Free Energy. At first thoughts seem to be thrown up as it were by the centrifugal force of the sensation, but if we allow them to fly past us and Disappear into Space we would Discover that it is the cyclic nature of our thoughts rather than the sensation that is the cause of our dis-ease. When we can *simply Be with* the sensation of our emotion and experience it fully at the non-conceptual level, we will notice a dynamic reversal taking place. The spinning energy that seemed to be generating ideas and rivulets of words has a *Still-Centre* like the 'eye' of a whirlwind. From that Experience of Stillness we can perceive that the obsessive spinning is not caused by the emotional sensation but is the cause of it. When we Realise the Empty or Spacious Nature of the sensation of emotional pain, the pain Dissolves into an *Ecstatic Sensation* of *Presence* and *Awareness*.

Throughout the ages people have attempted to describe the experience of Enlightenment, and the results have either been too simple, too complex, too obscure, too personal or too consummately poetic. But the only way to understand what is alluded to by such words as Enlightenment, Liberation or Realisation is through personal Experience. There is no sudden breakthrough that remains forever – there are only sudden glimpses. But the glimpses encourage us to see more, and so gradually we develop the ability to Integrate these Experiences of Unconditioned Being with our lives. Complete Integration of the Unconditioned State with every moment of our Being is Complete Enlightenment. The process of Being in the Moment Now enables us to work with our emotions and through doing so to Discover our Beginningless Enlightened Nature.

When we Recognise that we are becoming angry and we have developed sufficient confidence in View, we can Stare at our anger and Experience it as the Wisdom of Clarity.

When we Recognise that we are stiffening with pride or arrogance we can Stare at that haughtiness and Experience it as Equanimity and Equality.

When we Recognise that we are becoming frenzied by grasping desire we can stare at our wanting and Experience it as the Discriminating Awareness of Compassion.

When we Recognise that we are tightening with suspicion and jealousy we can Stare at our paranoia and Experience it as the Wisdom of Self-Accomplishing Action.

When we Recognise that we are obscuring ourselves in depression we can Stare at that overwhelming sensation and experience it as Brilliant Pervasive Intelligence in All-Encompassing Space.

This is by no means an instantaneous cure, but it is an Immediately Effective Method. Failure is the name of the game when it comes to attempting what is usually thought of as impossible. But Success is also the name of the game, right from the beginning. Every time we try to Stare into the face of our arising emotions we Confirm ourselves in the practice of cutting through our conditioning.

Even wanting to start is a success. Even a first failed attempt is a success, because in a very real sense there is no such thing as a bad meditation session – we learn something as long as we remain Open to Learning. So this must be our attitude – we are bound both to fail and succeed many times rather like the salmon that have to leap up waterfalls to reach their spawning grounds. Trying to change a lifetime of internal and external conditioning is a difficult task but not an impossible one. Unlike the salmon's though, our journey can be a little more joyous – if we begin to practise we will be able to experience a difference in our lives. The Ultimate Goal is always both very close and very distant, and when one day we come to realise that the Path *is* the Goal the concepts of failure and success will have no meaning.

Naturally, those of us who have some experience of meditation will be able to use this method with greater success than those of us who have never attempted this kind of thing. But whatever our experience is, waves of negative emotion can be a spur to practice if our perception of them allows disenchantment with the habits of distracted-being. We all have our own capacities and there is no saying whether people who have sat in practice over a period of time will do any better than fresh practitioners confronting their emotions directly for the first time. Motivation is absolutely necessary, and without the firm decision to work Directly with our emotions even those who feel they have meditative experience will get nowhere. It is sad to reflect on the number of people engaged in spiritual practice and the number of people who are actually prepared to work on themselves as they are in an everyday setting. For some people the Tibetan Mystic Path may as well be some sort of quirky esoteric hobby. If we are to engage in this kind of practice then it should be of some benefit to us. If we merely adopt a 'mystic outlook', fill our lives with oriental ritual observations and our vocabularies with oriental words and spiritual catch-phrases then all we are doing is filling time. We would do better to involve ourselves in voluntary work.

Basically, if the practice makes sense and if its purpose and function are understood, then results will be experienced and progress will ensue. In order to keep up this practice it has to *make sense* on a real *experiential level*. If the View presented here never becomes Lived-Knowledge then we will not be equipped with the carrying power to follow through and maintain the practice consistently in our lives.

In order to get some better idea of how we operate as people, 'feed-back' is very useful. Other people's views of us, although they cannot be wholly reliable, can be regarded as at least as real or as unreal as our own views of ourselves. Some people may like to imagine that they are misunderstood, and I'm sure that quite probably a few of them actually are, but in general most people have us summed up reasonably well especially if we take a concensus of their views. It is for this reason that counselling, guided encounter-group work and growth exercises within the framework of Tibetan Tantric Psychology can be very useful. These are methods which help a great deal to encourage our Openness and are important to our practice. The blending of techniques from our culture with the Tibetan Mystic Path under the right circumstances can become a powerful method for transforming our lives and creating a real bridge between the methods we are inheriting from Tibet and the place where we're going to practise them.

If we are successful in the practice of Staring at our negative emotions and we have become enthusiastic about the possibilities of this practice, then it is also possible to treat our pleasurable experiences in the same way. It is generally easier to learn from sorrow than from joy so most people are content to let happiness be rather than to risk it in any way. Real Joy and Well-Being, however, are not threatened by the Keenness of our Staring. Radiance is based on taking *Insecurity* as our *Security*, so if our pleasure is Real we Experience it as Complete Vibrant Awareness that extends itself Infinitely outward to all Beings.

This method is based on the Tibetan Tantric method called 'Zap-Lam', in which emotions are deliberately generated in order to Stare at them. Zap-Lam (the Profound Path of Realising the Co-emergence of Spaciousness and Ecstasy) includes the much misunderstood and much wondered-about practice of sexual Tantra. There have been numerous bizarre theories published on this theme ranging from the idea that it constitutes a test of ultimate lack of interest in sexual arousal to the idea that it is some sort of degenerate practice that has taken the Yab-Yum (Father-Mother) symbolism too literally. Sexuality is a vital part of our lives and as such is as Open to Mystic transformation as any other part of life. In Tibet there were celibate and non-celibate lineages and each structured their methods of practice according to different standpoints. The celibate monastic path is based on the Sutras of the Great Vehicle (Mahayana) which stress external renunciation as the means of Inner Transformation. The advantages of the choiceless life-style with its many rules and regulations are that the practitioner (nun or monk) gains a Sheer Simplicity of Living that enables her or him to avoid the otherwise almost unavoidable complication of the life of choices. The non-celibate path is based on the Tantras of the Thunderbolt Path (Vajrayana) which stress internal renunciation as a means of transforming life circumstances into Realisation on the Path. The advantages of external choice are that the practitioner Opens her or himself up to the richness of Life and all its multifarious opportunities.

One Path offers simplicity at the expense of richness of experiential possibilities. The other Path offers the wealth of life's experiences but with it come the wealth of complications that can sometimes be rather overwhelming. Neither Path is an easy one to take, but then living life as most of us do isn't that easy either. So sexuality is part of our experience of life, but any idea that we could 'get into' Tantric sex in the same way that we could 'get into' seeing a good film, is, sad to say, farcical. I'm sure most us could sit down and listen to a great symphony, but how many of us could write one? The answer of course is that everyone could write a great symphony but first we'd have to devote some effort to learning music. Suffice it to say the dealing with powerful energies requires powerful abilities on the part of the practitioner. In order to engage in the real practice of Zap-lam it is vital to be able to maintain the Mystic-Commitment to sustain Ro-chig (the one taste of Spaciousness and Ecstasy). The Essence of this and related practices is to Generate Sensation and then take that Sensation as the subject/object of meditation. This Sensation is then realised as the Liberated Energy of Self-Luminous Primordial Wisdom.

If sexuality is part of our lives then there is no harm in people learning to let go of 'themselves' a little and experiencing more *Unconstrained Warmth* for each other that is not based on selfish gratification. But if we deliberately arouse anger or any negative emotion and fail to Realise its Empty Nature we are left with the unhelpful perceptual patterning of whatever emotion it was that we aroused unnecessarily. Every time life *triggers* us and our potential for manifesting a powerful negative emotion is released we increase the distorted power of that potentiality.

If we repeat an action many times we become skilled in that action whatever it is. Even if we repeatedly make a mistake in our action we could say that we have become skilled in making that mistake.

The term 'skill' is obviously being used in a neutral manner and does not pertain to ideas of craftsmanship. I'll illustrate this with a memory from my days at art college. In my first year I should have gone along every Tuesday evening to learn how to type, but I was excused because I was one of those unfortunates who had already becomed 'skilled' at two-finger typing. Experience had shown the instructor that it was very difficult to teach anyone to type once they had taught themselves to type with two fingers – too much 'unlearning' was required. In any skill there are bad habits that we can easily 'learn' which will inhibit our advancement. In the *Skill* of unlearning our unenlightenment it's better to avoid picking up unskilful habits. Whether we are learning to drive a car, play a cello or work with our emotions it's fairly crucial not to develop counterproductive skills.

We find ourselves with all our emotions arising on a day to day basis whatever we do. We don't really need to deliberately arouse any emotion on top of those we experience every day. We've got our work cut out for us as it is.

I wish everyone reading this my very warmest encouragement on their Path and hope that everyone everywhere will eventually make the Journey into Vastness.

Element	Colour	Initial Reaction to Space	Distorted Energy	Liberated Energy	Direction	Season	Time	Khandro
Earth	Yellow	insubstantiality, hollowness, insecurity, fragility	obduracy, arrogance, pride, fixity, wilfulness, poverty/miserliness	Equality Equanimity, Balance, Harmony Wealth/Generosity	South	Autumn	Mid-morning	Rinchen
Water	White	fear (of direct recognised threats)	anger, aggression, hatred, violence	Clarity, Mirror-Wisdom, Penetrating Insight	East	Winter	Dawn/Sunrise	Dorje
Fire	Red	isolation, separation, desolation, loneliness	indiscriminate grasping possessiveness, obsessiveness compulsion, consumerism	Discriminating Wisdom, Compassion, Pure Appropriateness	West	Spring	Sunset	Pema
Air	Green	vulnerability, anxiety, nervousness, panic (at the feeling of susceptibility to indirect strategies)	envy, suspicion, jealousy, paranoia	Self-fulfilling Activity, Spontaneous Accomplishment, Free and Fluid Capacity for Action	North	Summer	Dusk/Early Night	Lekyi
Space	Blue	bewilderment (at being overpowered, overawed and overwhelmed by Spaciousness)	intentional ignorance, deliberate torpor, wilful stupidity, introversion, depression	Infinite Unrestricted Intelligence, Pervasive Wisdom, Omniscience	Central, Peripheral, Pervasive, Directionlessness	Time, Continuity	Timelessness	Sang-gye

Circle

APPENDIX I

The Calligraphies

Lama Sogyal Rinpoche, Tai Situ Rinpoche and Chögyam Trungpa Rinpoche have each been a tremendous inspiration and influence in the way that the art of Script-symbol has developed with me.

I was originally taught to write the Tibetan script by my adopted Brother and Sister, Dr Pema Dorjee and his wife Yeshi Khadro who are both very fluent and precise calligraphers. They both gave me, unstintingly, hours of their time from my first clumsy attempts to the smiles they gave me when I'd written the characters to their satisfaction.

I would often work by candlelight in the evenings when the only other source of light was that emanated by Yeshi la's kerosene stove on which she'd be frying up some tse-cho-cho (vegetables and noodles) for our evening meal. I remember one such night toward the end of the winter rains when the intermittent lightning was almost a better light source than the guttering candles. Amji Pema la would be sitting with his last patient of the day, taking the pulses and asking diagnostic questions that were periodically drowned out by the booming rolls of thunder that are so much louder among the mountains than they are anywhere else. Little wonder the Tibetans call thunder the voice of the dragon. On the plains it rolls high in the sky above you, but that's exactly where you are in the mountains. During the time I was with them in Mcleod Ganj and in Katmandu, they taught me the U-chen Tsugs, the Great headed-script which is used in the carving of texts onto wooden printing blocks. Writing these characters became such a pleasure and fascination to me that I filled many sheets of paper with what must have added up to several hundred thousand Ngak (mantras or awareness-spells). I used to make presents of these to fill the Mani-khorlos, the 'wish-path' wheels that the older Tibetans especially love to spin as they walk to and from the market.

Later, my great friend the Ven. Thubten Dadak showed me how to write in the U-med Tsugs, the cursive without-head style. Lama Sogyal Rinpoche had advised me that for my purposes the U-med style would prove more fluid and adaptable, but the almost entirely different alphabet was difficult to learn especially as there are several different forms of it. Thubten la had endless patience over hours of checking the new shapes that were unfamiliar to my hand. Thubten la is one of the saintliest people I have ever known and I was always deeply moved by his genuine humbleness and good heart. When my writing was obviously utterly appalling he'd say: "Yes, good, from this you start and become excellent." And when my writing was passable he'd say: "Oh, Chögyam la, this is very wonderful." He always seemed so pleased by every minor improvement that I made.

Each script has a living personality or character of its own that merges only when writing with reasonable skill and dexterity at sufficient speed for the hand to dance. Getting that somewhat magical sense of flow was elusive.

The Tibetan scripts go back a long way into the past. U-chen was devised around AD 640 by King Srongtsen Gampo's minister Thonmi Sambhota who undertook the perilous journey to India to study the Sanskrit grammar and alphabet. Basing the Tibet U-chen script on the Sanskrit model made the work of translating texts from the languages of India and Ögyen somewhat less difficult.

U-med on the other hand is based on the ancient script of Zhan-Zhung, the pre-Buddhist civilisation that had its centre in the Kailash area of Tibet. The ancient script was called sMar-yig and in present times is referred to by Bonpo scholars as sMar-Tsugs or as Lha-bab-yi-ge which means 'script descended from the heavens', and is possibly over three thousand years old. Comparing the ancient script of sMar-yig with U-med Tsugs, U-chen Tsugs and Sanskrit it is quite easy to see (as Lama Namkhai Norbu Rinpoche points out) the individual derivations of the scripts and how they have influenced each other in Tibet.

My method of calligraphy has become very personal and individual in its development. I use a large Chinese calligraphy brush rather than a pen; and rather than the traditional ink block used with such a brush I prefer waterproof Indian ink because of the crisp edge it gives. I use the brush well saturated with ink on fully (though unevenly) sized hand-made rag paper from Sikkim. The Chinese and Japanese methods with which I'm also familiar utilise mainly a sparsely loaded brush on more absorbent papers. The results are different and intuitive experimentation has shown me my most natural means of spontaneous expression.

I spent a long time working on scrap paper, the backs of out-of-date medical calendars, and gradually covered the walls of my room with the marks I was making. It is traditional to burn or bury such attempts but times change and now the possibility of recycling paper at home makes possible an incredible variety of possibilities in terms of paper texture, colour and pattern.

The approach I adopted was to lay out a pile of scrap paper on top of a sheet of thick rough hand-made water-colour paper. The idea came from watching part of television documentary at the house of a friend. The documentary dealt with the uses of computers in industry, and one scene involved a computer-linked mechanical arm which was being 'taught' how to spray-paint a car body by an expert spray-painter who used the spraying arm guided by his hand to paint the car. Once programmed in this way the machine could proceed to expertly spray the next how-ever-many cars they decided to push through. I was not entirely happy about the prospect of unemployment that would undoubtedly arise from the development of such a device, but an idea dawned for a calligraphic approach.

If I could teach my hand and arm by continuous repetition to know how to produce a linked series of marks on paper then my conditioned sense of aesthetics would get sold short. I was quite excited about this method of no method – of selling my contrived judgemental faculties down the river. So I knelt before my pile of paper and, beginning very slowly, drew out a character over and over again, gradually increasing in speed until I'd completed the penultimate sheet. At that point I'd put aside the brush and enter into meditation. After a time I would take up the brush, charge it with ink and allow my hand to make the marks it *knew* how to make – I just followed on behind with suspended breath and eyes slightly out of focus.

A calligraphy is an act of self-disclosure – it hides nothing of what we are – so showing people your calligraphies is a bit like taking off your clothes. It's a naked presentation of what we are. The blank sheet of paper is an empty mirror in which we have the opportunity of *seeing* ourselves through the brush and ink.

This method worked well but the use of ink and paper proved a little ridiculous. On one occasion whilst sitting silently before the final sheet of paper the telephone rang and a new and humorous calligraphic approach evolved. I quickly dashed off the calligraphy before answering the phone.

I still continue to practise the characters many times in order to let my hand 'feel' their forms, but now I use a pen and work on a smaller scale on a single sheet. Once I have trained my hand to produce an accurate mark of its own accord, I get down to the washing up, clean the kitchen floor, begin to prepare a meal or do whatever needs to be done around the house. The doorbell and the telephone are regular interruptions at certain times of the day, so it is at those times that I choose to execute calligraphies. A single sheet of paper is left ready for use on the table with ink and brush poised. I forget about the calligraphy and get on with the housework until either the telephone or doorbell rings, and the calligraphy gets completed on the way to either summons.

I enjoy the way that the exact moment is taken completely out of my hands and the way that the calligraphy becomes part of my housework. There is no way of preparing yourself because it could just be one of those days when you're not interrupted for several hours. So you are faced squarely with what you are doing and how you happen to be feeling about it.

It was at this point that the splatters started occurring in the calligraphies. The speed at which the brush has to be charged en route to the door or phone makes it impossible to control the extent to which the brush is charged with ink. The result is that, almost invariably, droplets of ink fly from the brush in the haste of its movement to explode onto the calligraphy paper in limitless variety.

Having commissioned a set of five calligraphies from me, Rainbow called unexpectedly one day before I had completed them to my satisfaction. A few of the calligraphies were 'spoilt' by splatters, so I was most surprised when he adamantly refused to let me replace the 'spoilt' sheets with splatter-free pieces.

The sheer delight he'd expressed at the anarchic quality of the accidental splatters caused me to take a serious look at them. I sat and stared at them for some time after he'd gone – they certainly were very energetic and I could not help liking them. I tried to dissuade myself but by the time I stood up I knew that Rainbow was right. The splatters stayed.

I hope you will enjoy the calligraphies in this book as much as I have enjoyed being instrumental in their coming into Being.

NGAKPA CHÖGYAM
Roath, Cardiff, June 1985

APPENDIX II
Sources

My sources for the mystic, theoretic and cultural content of *Rainbow of Liberated Energy* are the Tibetan Lamas, the Nuns, Monks and Ngakpas listed below who so kindly presented their Teachings in discourses, interviews, books, pamphlets, transcripts, letters, conversations, initiations, transmissions, revelations and dreams. The sources are arranged in alphabetical order apart from the Heads of the Schools.

H.H. Dalai Lama
H.H. Dudjom Rinpoche
H.H. Sakya Trizin Rinpoche
H.H. Gyalwa Karmapa Rinpoche
Akong Rinpoche
Ani Pema Tsomo
Ani Pema Wangmo
Ani Tsultrim Zangmo
Ani Wangchuk
Ani Yeshe Kandro
Apo Rinpoche
Arnam Lama
Aro Rinpoche
Ato Rinpoche
Chatral Rinpoche
Chime Yönten Rinpoche
Chhimed Rigdzin Rinpoche
Chögyam Trungpa Rinpoche
Chögye Rinpoche
Chöje Gyatso Rinpoche
Dabzang Rinpoche
Deshung Rinpoche
Dilgo Kyentse Rinpoche
Dodropchen Rinpoche
Drukje Rinpoche
Drupön Rinpoche
Dzogchen Rinpoche
Gegen Khyentse Rinpoche
Geshe Damchö Yönten
Geshe Jampa Gyatso
Geshe Jampa Wangdü

Geshe Ngawang Dhargye
Geshe Rabten
Geshe Thekchok
Geshe Wangchen
Gomo Tulku
Gyaltsap Rinpoche
Jamgön Kongtrül Rinpoche
Jamyang Khandro
Jetsun Kushog Rinpoche
Jetsun Pema
Jigdral Dagchen Sakya Rinpoche
Kalu Rinpoche
Kangyur Rinpoche
Khamtrül Donju Nyima Rinpoche
Khamtrül Yeshe Dorje Rinpoche
Khensur Pema Gyaltsen Rinpoche
Khyentse Sangyum
Kunzung Dorje Rinpoche
Lama Ngawang Rinpoche
Lama Könchog Rinpoche
Luding Khen Rinpoche
Minling Trichen Rinpoche
Namkhai Norbu Rinpoche
Pawo Rinpoche
Phende Rinpoche
Ponlop Rinpoche
Rato Rinpoche
Sapchu Rinpoche
Sang-gye Nyenpa Tulku
Sang-gye Tendzin Jongdong Rinpoche
Shamar Rinpoche

Sogyal Rinpoche
Song Rinpoche
Tarthang Tulku
Thubten Dadak la
Thubten Yeshe Rinpoche
Thubten Zopa Rinpoche
Traleg Rinpoche
Trangu Rinpoche

Trijang Rinpoche
Trinley Norbu Rinpoche
Trongsar Rinpoche
Trundgram Gyaldrul Rinpoche
Tsenshap Serkong Rinpoche
Tsering Lama
Tulku Pema Wangyal Rinpoche
Yongdzin Ling Rinpoche

Courses and Workshops

If having read *Rainbow of Liberated Energy* you would like to take your interest further, courses are held several times a year which use this book as 'core-material'.

Ngakpa Chögyam also gives experiental counselling courses based on the Colour and Element system of Tibetan Tantric Psychology. He leads group retreats, meditation courses, Shamanic workshops, and travels on invitation to other countries.

For further information on these courses and workshops, enquiries (enclosing a large stamped addressed envelope) should be addressed to:

The Secretary

"Sang-ngak-chö-dzong"

Tibetan Tantric Periphery

203, Arabella Street

Roath Park

Cardiff CF2 4SZ

Wales, U.K.

End – Tha (mTha')